Face to *Face*
with *Reality*

Face to Face with Reality

Questions of earnest spiritual seekers answered with
simplicity and clarity by a Realized Jnani

Rajini Menon

YogiImpressions®

YogiImpressions®

FACE TO FACE WITH REALITY
First published in India in 2014 by
Yogi Impressions Books Pvt. Ltd.
1711, Centre 1, World Trade Centre,
Cuffe Parade, Mumbai 400 005, India.
Website: www.yogiimpressions.com

First Edition, September 2014

Copyright © 2014 by Rajini Menon

Cover Design: www.designpinkindia.com

ISBN 978-93-82742-21-0

Printed at: Repro India Ltd., Mumbai

Contents

Swami Dayananda Saraswati

Commendation by
Swami Dayananda Saraswati

SWAMI DAYANANDA SARASWATI

[Handwritten note]

Smt. Rajini has given answers to questions commonly asked by people in her way, more often intuitively. Her thinking can inspire people to look at "What is" with a different, refreshing perspective.

10 5·13·

Arsha Vidya Gurukulam, Anaikatti (P O) Coimbatore 641 108 INDIA   Ph : + 91 422 265 7001 / 265 7007 Fax : + 91 422 265 7002
Swami Dayananda Ashram, Purani Jhadi, Rishikesh 249 201 Uttaranchal INDIA   Ph & Fax : + 91 135 243 0769 / 243 2769
Arsha Vidya Gurukulam, P O Box 1059, Saylorsburg, Pa., 18353 - 1059 USA   Ph : +1 570 992 2339 Fax : +1 570 992 7150 / 9617

Transcription: 'Smt. Rajini has given answers to questions commonly asked by people in her way, more often intuitively. Her thinking can inspire people to look at "What is" with a different, refreshing perspective.'

Commendation by
Swami Rajeswarananda Saraswati

While writing a commendation to this book and about Smt. Rajini Menon, the first thing that comes to mind is the attitude and approach about freedom or absolute truth by U. G. Krishnamurti: 'Truth, which is life itself, is like a living flame without shape – so don't try to bind it or imprison it with any definite forms, with any systems or religion, dogmas, doctrines and institutions. To do so is to kill it.' I had enough opportunities to interact with Smt. Rajini Menon. I can very well say that the expression of 'Truth' in Mrs. Menon is exceptional. She has a blossomed intelligence with pristine purity. I feel the fragrance of the gentle breeze which carries the beauty of truth and peace, which can attract people. Her words come from the innermost core.

She was a normal housewife till 2008, and until then had no exposure to spirituality. She had to face heart breaking situations and had to undergo unbearable pain which she handled by her tremendous inner strength and absolute righteousness following her inner voice. The whole transformation happened thus. The body system underwent various changes and finally the absolute truth dawned on her. Individual identity and personification vanished forever in a natural way. The system started functioning in the most natural, normal and beautiful way. All the concepts and conditionings were totally wiped out effortlessly. Pivotal point of circle got smashed. Thus, all the limitations got transcended and became one with the whole without boundary and barrier. Everything became spontaneous.

The transformation happened all of a sudden by the will of nature (God), and her body mechanism was shaken thoroughly paving the way to death experience just like that of Ramana Maharshi, UG, Ajja and many others. To regain normalcy it takes time, sometimes a very long time. But in her case normalcy was instantaneous and a new life started in tune with the cosmic consciousness. Ever since, she was spontaneous in answering questions of ardent, genuine and sincere seekers.

What flows out through her about life and truth are mesmerisingly grand. Whatever is the level of the seeker, she is seen to be coming down to their level. The flow of words enter their hearts, penetrating and shattering their ego. There is only spontaneity. This book is a compilation of such spontaneous answers to seekers.

To me she is wonderful and extraordinary for *satsang*. I have always felt tremendous peace, serenity and purity in her presence.

– Swami Rajeswarananda Saraswati,
Chief Editor, Rishimukh

Commendation by
Swami Gabheerananda

The 'Awakening' which resulted in Self-Realization graciously paved the way to Rajini's commendable insight and crystal clear dexterity a few years back. She has compassionately answered the questions that some true spiritual seekers and some common people have been asking. This is a wonderful compilation of many such conversations. The questions that have been put forth by spiritual aspirants about life, its purpose, and enlightenment were answered effortlessly. This is a very special book which brings you face to face with reality and throws light on everyone to live their life beautifully and righteously.

The actionless "I" was experienced in her total absorption, a few years ago. This is a rare phenomenon which happens on this planet. We are blessed to have such a soul amongst us. More wonderful are the words that have come out of such a Divine soul. They assure us of a light pointing towards the truth. All that flows out through her is very much in tune with Vedantic teachings and its perfection has been endorsed by a living legend, a living authority on *Vedanta*, who is also my Guru – Swami Dayananda Saraswati.

May this book attain its maximum purpose by the all-merciful Self. My prayers and blessings.

– Swami Gabheerananda
Acharya, Chinmaya Mission

Foreword

Rajini Menon is truly a most remarkable woman. An ordinary householder, she has attained Self-Realization and her writings, which are largely answers to questions sent to her by spiritual aspirants, illustrate that she is undoubtedly a Jnani Guru. How did this miracle happen? She says she received this great blessing from *purva janma sukritham* i.e. from a previous life.

Did Rajini perform any *sadhanas* or spiritual practices in this birth? The answer is a definite 'No'. But if you talk to her, she says her life itself was nothing less than an intense sadhana. She had got the *janma vasana* or instinctive desire to abide strongly by her inner voice or the 'Inner Divine' voice from her previous birth. This was the only light that always guided her on an evolutionary path into higher consciousness. She says that her inner journey was in absolute aloneness and darkness. Stumbling, hitting here and there, falling, getting injured and undergoing intense pain, till she found herself in the light. We can feel the intensity and hardships she went through on her journey without an external Sadguru. Though outwardly she was alone all through her journey, she held onto the 'Inner Divine' tightly without loosening her hold on it.

Self-Realization from a previous life is very rare, but there are the recent precedents of Ramana Maharshi who on being asked how he attained enlightenment at the age of sixteen replied, 'It must have been in a previous life.' Similarly, Anandamayi Ma said, 'I was born awake,' and later demonstrated all the sadhanas that she had performed in a previous life.

This miracle happened to Rajini Menon much later in life when she was an employed householder and a housewife. She is a simple, humble lady, now aged forty-seven, who leads a very ordinary life. She is readily available for a genuine spiritual aspirant, or whom *prakruti* brings to her. She does not do anything in the way of reaching out to teach anyone. She simply goes with nature's flow with all her heart and a great deal of compassion for all who come to see her, or write to her. Whatever flows from her replies is merely an expression of her love. She is generally silent and would appear to be like any lady next door. Only a very few have recognised her gifted inner resources. To those who visit her, she helps them through the hurdles they face in their spiritual search and her answers are most profound and quite spontaneous. Spiritual aspirants have felt their knots to be loosened and untied. Her life is basically restricted to her home and office. Whenever she speaks, it is a reflection of her life and righteous living that is always her main underlying inspiration. She is a courageous, mentally strong woman who under all circumstances abides by the voice of the 'Inner Divine' inspiration along with her discriminative powers. Before her sudden 'awakening' on the 18th of July 2008, she was just another ordinary person who could or would speak nothing along the lines of that which she now does. She neither had any exposure to the so-called spiritual world, nor studied Vedanta or any spiritual books. She herself wonders at the spontaneous flow that happens through her. In brief, she is an ordinary householder who does not conduct any official satsangs. The few who came to know her were spiritual aspirants who reached out to her, and she replied to them through correspondence.

Incidentally, one of her relatives is an evolved soul around 70 years of age, and well-versed in the *shastras*. He is one of the very few persons who first recognised her special gifts because he was aware that she knew absolutely nothing about religious scriptures before 2008. From then on she was able to explain any questions regarding deep spiritual matters with tremendous clarity and wisdom. So, one or two spiritual seekers who were close to him also came to know about her as well. She doesn't claim she is enlightened and nobody in her neighbourhood knows that she is a transformed human being. She does not claim to be or act as a teacher. It's only when some sincere seekers or questioners come to her that she is compassionate enough to answer them and resolve their difficulties. Her answers flow spontaneously and are directed to the needs of the person before her. It is by a very rare bestowal of Divine Grace that this event of Self-Realization happened to her.

She has kindly given permission for this book to be

compiled to assist spiritually inclined readers. For this generosity on her part, we are truly grateful. She has a beautiful, expressive face that has an innocent, childlike quality about it. It can well be said that her life itself is an internal *tapasya* or intense sadhana not known to the outside world.

What more need be said? This remarkable woman's attainment speaks more powerfully than words can express. They tell us that here, once more, a true Jnani Guru has appeared on this perplexed planet. It is hoped that her answers to questions, given with such depth of understanding and clarity, will help earnest aspirants proceeding on the spiritual path. Such great beings are very rare on earth, and I am sure her words will help those readers who are searching for the Ultimate Truth. Rajiniji has said many times that the existence of 'such beings' is not as rare as those who can recognise them – a profound paradox indeed.

Her writing is simple, clear and full of compassion. It touches the heart with its beautiful flow. Since she is so pure and compassionate, she comes to the questioner's level. Her answers are often elaborate explanations, looking at issues from several different angles, and they are complete in themselves. She covers the whole range of spiritual queries that usually confront an earnest seeker on the spiritual path. She mainly focuses on the principles of *Advaita,* Vedanta and *Dvaita*. She even tackles the thorny question of atheism with astonishing skill and precision. She also discusses the process of Self-Enquiry and Ramana Maharshi's infallible way to Self-Realization. She has made several visits to Ramanasramam in Tiruvannamalai after 2008.

A great surprise is her description of a poem by Henry Wadsworth Longfellow. She explained to me how she came to write this commentary. When after her transformation, her daughter came up to her to understand this poem, the meaning came to her spontaneously and she wrote it down. The next day, when her daughter showed the meaning to her English teacher, the teacher asked her if her mother's subject was Literature and if she taught English. In this precious book, Rajini covers the whole gamut of questions that may arise on one's spiritual journey. The fact that her words have been endorsed by a great Vedic authority like Sri Dayananda Swami speaks for itself. I have nothing more to offer in this respect except to say that Divine Grace has led us to a remarkable woman whose knowledge will prove to be of great benefit to all those who read this most worthy book.

The details of her remarkable spiritual awakening in her own words in the 'Introduction' after the Preface, should be carefully read as a unique testament to her profound wisdom and knowledge. Furthermore, Rajini Menon has kindly and graciously agreed to answer any serious questions about the sadhana and spiritual journey of earnest readers of her book. You may communicate with her through email: 4trueseekers@gmail.com

– Alan Jacobs, President
Ramana Maharshi Foundation, UK
London, July 2014

Preface

To begin with I am grateful to Alan Jacobs, President of the Ramana Maharshi Foundation UK, and author of many profound spiritual books and poetry, for guiding and helping me organise and categorise the compiled answers to questions by Rajiniji, whom I call Amma, with great reverence and affection. This book contains her spontaneous answers to those spiritual aspirants who have contacted her for spiritual guidance, mainly through email and internet spiritual forums, on how to progress in their spiritual quest. There are no words to describe the simplicity, clarity and compassion with which she answers their questions. She says that it is prakruti that chooses those who are ready to receive the right message, at the right time, in the right way, and at the right place.

A couple of years ago when I was engaged in an intense period of spiritual quest, it was by the Grace of the Divine that I found Amma. She is the personification of compassion. I have never met another human being like her who is a living symbol of purity, as Divinity flows from her. Her simplicity, her down to earth ways and childlike innocence, captured my mind and heart. She is a courageous woman with an unbelievable mental strength. Selflessness and fearlessness are other features that define her. One principle that she has never compromised in her life, both before and after her transformation, is righteousness in her everyday living. Whatever the cost she has had to pay for being righteous, she has never forsaken these honourable principles.

Her life has been full of hardship and painful events but she always blesses those who have been instrumental in causing her pain. She prays for their well-being and happiness. She feels they are all privileged souls who have been instrumental in lifting her upwards in her evolutionary process, and expresses her gratitude towards them. She has also told me that most of the time the realities are known only to her 'Inner Divine', and not even to the immediate person involved, as she remains silent and absorbs everything in herself. She will also go to the extent of shouldering someone else's mistakes upon herself either voluntarily, or at times silently, which are imposed on her knowingly by others.

As a child, just before going off to sleep every night, she used to reflect on the entire day's activities. She would then identify all those thoughts and actions which her inner conscience would not approve. She would instruct herself never to repeat such feelings again. This was a continuous process until she found herself thinking and doing everything in accordance with her inner conscience. This introspection, analysis, and corrective measures were part of her life, secretly happening within herself.

In her words, she says that, "Rajini was someone who was once very dear to her." It is only after a great deal of persuasion that she will reveal a little of her past, or as she puts it, 'Rajini's life'.

I have been greatly benefited by her presence and her words on my spiritual journey, and I hope to receive even more benefit from her words in my quest. I am ever grateful to the Divine Grace that she personifies. I cannot adequately describe the great darkness I was in, before I came to her lotus feet, and how much light I now have in my life. Neither can I describe the intense longing that I had for such Divine Grace in any form, and the burning pain that I was experiencing, not knowing what to do and where to go. In the past, I had been searching through the internet, contacting many Gurus, and making friends with several persons who were spiritually evolved. I realized that all of them had in many ways helped me evolve to a level where I could receive the Grace that Amma exemplifies. I am thankful to all of them and all the spiritual writings of mature and realized souls whom I have studied. I realize this is High Grace that the Divine has bestowed upon me.

Thanks to the Divine for having brought me to a rare soul like Alan Jacobs, who is able to recognise Amma and share his feelings through writing the Foreword to this book and helping it see the light. My grateful thanks go out to His Holiness Swami Dayananda Saraswati, the greatest living authority on Vedanta today, for his appreciation and validation of Rajini. My grateful thanks also go out to both Swami Rajeswarananda Saraswati and

Swami Gabheeranandaji for their valuable commendations on this book and its author. I also thank all the true and genuine seekers who have approached Amma with their genuine questions through which there was this grand flow of *jnanam*. This compilation is submitted at the lotus feet of Amma, the Divine, with tears of gratitude.

– Dr. Santhosh Narayanan
Asst. Professor,
State University of New York, USA.

Rajini Menon

Introduction

On the 18th of July 2008, something unusual happened to Rajini Menon. Everything was released from her heart, she felt all the knots dissolving, and a blissful state arising from there. She had just moved into her bedroom and sat with legs folded on the bed, her back straight, eyes closed. The children were studying in the other room, they sensed that she was disturbed, and they never disturbed her at such times. It was 7.30 in the evening and the lights were off in her room. Her attention went to a spot slightly towards the right side, a bit lower to the centre of her chest, and a single thought prevailed there that, 'I am this *Atma* here, with no name and form.'

It just so happened that the last remnants of the mind were cast off totally from her and then there was absolutely nothing that she had to think about. Probably, her system had foreseen that thinking would extinguish her. Then a stillness spread through her entire being. From that stillness arose a blissful state. She experienced an unbearable joy

1

and felt weightless as though she was floating. She could not feel the presence of her body; a limitless expanse occurred. She does not know how long she was lost in that state. From then on, she could enter that state of stillness any time she wished. The first thought that came to her after she came out of that thoughtless state was, 'Oh! The whole world is in grief for no reason. If this simple secret is shared with all, everyone can come out of grief and be blissful.' The other thing that was observed was that there were no questions left in her.

That was the day when the transformation happened and the last thought still clinging to her heart was dropped. She had reached the brim of that maturity level and was thus blessed by Divine Grace and transformed. That was probably the last knot-entanglement remaining that was removed. From then on she has been living in a liberated state. Nothing ever has touched 'Self' since then. Her life totally changed, although nothing changed. One can say it was an overnight event, but it was actually never so. It was in fact a process that was taking place every second of her life, and the completion was overnight. Ever since, there has only been a state of pure wonderment.

Before this final change occurred, there were some happenings in her life that are worth mentioning. It was in February 2008 that she happened one night to see her dead body on the marbled floor, in the moonlight. The body, though decked up beautifully, was lying there dead and she asked herself, 'Who is lying here?' There came a spontaneous correction in the question as 'What is it?' in place of 'Who is this?' And the answer came spontaneously,

'This is the food for worms'.

Later, in the months of April and May 2008, she transformed completely into the Divine where Rajini was not allowed to be present at all. This was an inevitable process in her life, as Rajini was incapable of handling situations righteously, in those tough situations when her being righteous would mean she would be shattered to pieces, and the only way out for her to be righteous was by driving Rajini out and letting the 'Inner Divine' function through her. This was intentionally done every minute of her waking state as her presence could, that very minute, shatter her into pieces. The one easy way out available to her was to shun righteousness and that would let her breath continue. But then all that was possible only if she, in some corner of her heart, found it agreeable to do that. It was only after surviving this intense period that the final transformation happened.

It is inevitable for a pure soul to undergo difficult situations in life, which are really blessings of the Divine. It is not easy to handle these tough situations in a righteous way. It is here that the real test comes. Holding on to the Divine may lead to your own death and if you still hold on, it is only out of sheer unconditional love for the Divine. It is in this situation of holding on to the Divine even when the very holding on to can lead to an encounter with death, that the Divine appears face to face. It takes over everything and you disappear. What is left is an embodiment of *Dharma*. This is the point where you overcome death and the real birth happens – the Realization of the real 'I'.

CHAPTER 1

Secrets Of Life

Karma

Q: Why am I born on this earth and what is the goal or purpose of my life?

Rajini: All of us are born on this earth because of our past karma. The causes of unpleasant experiences now are due to our bad karma in the past. All the pleasant experiences are due to our good karma in the past.

We are in fact born on this earth only to experience these pleasant and unpleasant experiences. When we come to know this secret, who would not feel a ripple of joy? We experience unpleasant experiences because by undergoing all those unpleasant and painful experiences, we are actually clearing off all our past accounts of bad karma or adharma.

The revelation of this secret also enlightens us about another fact: we should be careful not to have any negative or bad *Adharmic* feelings or thoughts, speak hateful words, or perform any actions which would lead to further accumulation of bad karma and, in turn, undergo further painful experiences in the future. This means the moulding of our future is truly in our hands. Do you see the beauty of this? Thus each second of our life should be spent in reducing all negative karma from our accounts by experiencing all the pain, with due gratitude to the person who has been instrumental in creating the painful situation for us. We should be grateful to God for being kind enough, for creating the situations to clear off all the negative karma of the past. At the same time, all efforts should be made on our part to add more good karma in our account, so that we experience pleasant and joyful experiences in the future.

What exactly are we doing here on earth? We must know that very clearly without any confusion.

Q: *How to recognise and complete prarabdha karma?*

Rajini: Why do we experience painful situations in life? It's all because of our past karma. The past indicates all the past – either in this life, or in previous births. By experiencing or undergoing the pain, we are actually diminishing our past accounts of bad actions. By diminishing those accounts we are actually nearing God, provided that in the process of experiencing we do not create any further bad karma.

Whatever be the negativity, pain, sadness, anxiety or stress that we experience in life, the first thing that must enter our mind should be the feeling of internal joy of being the ones who know the truth of Nature's laws of causation. That very moment, we must internally realize that God has bestowed upon us His Grace and Blessings so that our past bad karma is washed away.

How do you think we ought to handle the clearance of clutter? Should we allow any further increase in bad karma in our accounts? Suppose we are reducing 10 marks worth of bad karma from our accounts and in the process if we land up increasing the net worth of bad karma to 15 or so, then what is the use? Are you seeing the point?

Now, what acts of ours would increase bad karma?

Suppose we undergo pain worth 10 marks and while undergoing this we, by doing some vengeful acts towards that person who happens to cause the pain, incur say 12 marks of bad karma. Then after undergoing pain worth 10 marks, you are left with a net gain of 12 marks of bad karma.

In case you are not a vengeful sort of person and you do not take any revenge, but you speak ill of him to his face, then maybe you will only incur about say 8 marks of bad karma. The net effect you are left with after undergoing 10 marks of pain is just 8, as against 12 in the previous instance.

Now, let us consider what happens if you don't speak ill of that person to his face, but express the very same feelings to someone you are close to? You would then incur about 6 marks of bad karma and, while you are reducing your 10 marks of bad karmas by undergoing all the pain, your net balance now is to the extent of 6. Do you see that? You would in effect be left with 6 marks worth of pain to be experienced in the future.

Maybe you don't speak ill of that person to anyone, but secretly harbour some ill feelings for him. For example, let's say you can never digest how a person for whom you have wholeheartedly been doing all good can be so unkind and ruthless to you. Now, though good at heart, but being an emotional sort, you land up harbouring such bad feelings in your heart although outwardly you behave well and still do good for him. Such a person would, in the process of reducing his share of 10 points of pain, further add only 2 points. In future, he would only have to undergo 2 more points of pain in order to clear off his account.

Let's talk of another person who does not have any ill feelings at heart and believes that the pain he undergoes is his share alone and something which is inevitable. This man is not incurring any more points of bad karma and is clearing away all his 10 points. Now he is left with a clean slate.

Yet another person, who though undergoing pain, still has sympathetic, loving and caring feelings for the one who has been instrumental in inflicting the pain. He or she, in addition, feels grateful and thankful towards him, as he had been instrumental in reducing the 10 bad karma points of his past. But for this kind act of that person, he would never have been able to diminish the pending bad karma. Do you see that? So, this man continues having all the good feelings, thoughts, words, and acts as he sees the Divine in him. What do you think his balance sheet would show? It would shoot up from a clear −10, to a positive figure of say +2 or +4 or +16 and so on. The leaps would be in geometric progression towards the positive side, unlike the slow changes that were taking place in the balance sheet till now. An increase on the positive side would again by the very same laws of causation, be bound to bestow a great deal of joy upon you.

Whether we know the truth or not, events invariably will follow the ever abiding laws of cause and effect. The ignorant one in his ignorance, even while undergoing the experiences of pain, instead of reducing the portions experienced keeps increasing the amount of balance left for experiencing. This negativity also shoots up in geometric progression, as this vicious cycle of undergoing pain keeps recurring. And out of ignorance, one lands up further increasing the accounts of bad karma.

Take the example of one who is ignorant and is seen outwardly doing good and speaking good out of his inability to oppose the one who is inflicting pain, for want of courage or out of sheer tolerance, so that the problem is not further aggravated. What do you think would be his plight? Here, the world might see him to be one, equal to the One, whose veils of ignorance have all been removed. But in reality it is not so. In this case there is frustration brewing inside but it is being bottled up, and this goes a long way in the creation of our vasanas – the very nature that we have from birth. In this case, you are born with the very tendencies that were being suppressed in your behaviour. These tendencies were not being seen because they were being suppressed. So you see that suppression is an even more dangerous tendency. It doesn't leave you even after death; it follows to your next birth as well.

The grip it has is a strong one. These vasanas can create fresh bad karma for us.

By now you must have realized the importance of knowing relative truths and the laws of cause and effect. Understanding these laws of causation well, imbibing them without any doubts, churning them intermittently in your mind, and practicing them in your life is sadhana. These are efforts (*purusharthas*) we have to make during all our waking hours in all that we indulge in, because the vasanas that we have to overpower are the ones that have travelled a long way with us, from the many births that we have previously experienced. Despite all your efforts, these vasanas would still keep cropping up out of habit. When you realize that the vasanas have cropped up, give them some time to wean off. The more you churn the laws of causation in your mind and determine to practice things the righteous way, the more strongly you will be able to overpower the vasanas. Success lies in frequent churning of these truths about the laws of cause and effect.

I repeat: Success lies in how often and how well you do the churning of the truth in the mind.

Q: Does the mind of other people who live together also change, or does that depend on their prarabdha ?

Rajini: To answer your question, the other person's behaviour and attitude towards you would change with the change in your attitude! The time required for the change towards you would depend on your prarabdha karma, and the time required for a change otherwise would depend on their prarabdha karma.

10

As you proceed with this new attitude in life, don't let any doubts remain. Whatever be the doubts, ask freely without any hesitation. They will be removed. There is neither any difficulty nor anything to hinder our life in any way, in this new attitude towards life. Everything about life would be more joyful. Be assured. Gradually, everything will be taken care of by the Divine residing in your heart. You will be able to see Him guiding you always!

CHAPTER 2

Inner Voice: The Divine Guidance

On Life

Q: What is Life?

Rajini: Life is very simple. There is nothing complicated about life. Life means just this moment. No two people in the world share the same moment. This moment is exclusively yours. Now, what does this moment consist of? This moment consists of you and what comes to you in this moment – does it not? So, life is this moment and it consists of you and what comes to you in the moment.

So, how should you handle this moment? You have to first accept what comes to you in the moment. What is acceptance? Acceptance is to mentally acknowledge that such and such situation is here and now. After fully accepting it this way, the next step is to do what is the most righteous thing to do in the situation, whatever be the situation. And what is this most righteous thing to be done? How can one know that? The most righteous act will be what your inner voice or conscience – *manasakshi* – tells you, and not what your mind tells you. How do you differentiate between the true inner voice and the mind's outer voice?

If you are served a bowl of apples and also a dish of sweets, and if you are diabetic with a craving for sweets, your 'mind' will pull you towards eating the sweets but your inner voice will tell you to go for the apples. Now, suppose a bowl of apples and a basket of oranges are put before you. If your mind draws you towards oranges and your inner voice will be agreeing with it, then either of these choices will be right. That is to say, if there is a conflicting voice within you that is an opposing voice between the inner and the outer voice, you have to listen to and follow the inner voice. Where there is no conflict between the inner and the outer voice, you may follow your whim and fancy of that moment. Your confusion is over once you accept what comes to you and choose what will be the right thing to do in that situation.

In a nutshell, if you look at life there is nothing more to it than this moment, and handling this moment in the most righteous way.

Q: How can I lead a peaceful life?

Rajini: Life is always peaceful; nothing other than peace exists. When there is only peace, what is the point of asking 'how to lead a peaceful life'? What advice can be given when there is nothing other than peace? There is only peace and nothing else.

What makes life unpeaceful? It is ignorance that veils this peace. Removing ignorance is the best way out of this dilemma. Who has to remove it and from whom? How can peace search for peace, when there is nothing other than peace?

Your question implies that it is someone else looking for peace. The one who is looking for peace is the one called 'i' – isn't that so? Who is that? Had peace been that 'i', there would be no need to look for peace. Therefore, something non-existent is looking for peace. How is that possible? Think! The cause of all this confusion is the veil of ignorance covering the truth. When the veils of ignorance are shed, all that remains is only peace. So remove the veils of ignorance and then discover 'who' this remover truly is. Then peace alone will be left.

On Righteous Living

Q: A customer shouted at me for a petty reason. He was talking loudly on his cell phone and disturbing my work at the counter. I politely asked him to refrain from talking so loudly as I did not feel any ill feeling towards him. Since such disturbances cannot be encouraged in an office, I sought advice from my Branch Manager who said that probably the person was denied some unjust demand by the Bank and that made him react in this manner. I would like to ask you if I am moving in the right direction?

Rajini: Think of both situations: when you react to a person or a situation in a tit-for-tat manner and, on the other hand, when you simply act in a way that is right irrespective of what and how the other person reacts. In which of the two situations do you have peace of mind?

In the first case, if you were to give tit-for-tat it would keep disturbing you. In the second case, you are at peace because your mind is focusing on what is the right response you should give and not on the outcome of your actions. In this case, you remain unaffected by the other person's behaviour because you understand you have control only over your actions. What others do is their action and not yours, so why should you be disturbed or affected?

When someone tells you how dare that fellow talk to you like this, then you can tell yourself 'Oh, did he really talk to me like that? It never occurred to me in the first place!' Then ignore it with some comforting thought by telling yourself, 'He must be having some problems and may God help him sort them out.' In this way, you will have successfully dealt with the situation and this is real growth for you as a mature individual. This is steadily going up the ladder.

The first thing to be understood is that if you engage in tit-for-tat, your mind will be disturbed, but when you act by listening to your inner voice – you will be at peace. In the same situation if you had answered back with irritation, you would not be deriving that inner joy which you will get out of having handled the situation without being affected by external irritants, and of being able to maintain the righteousness in your behaviour. This leads to joy emanating from inside as it is the activation of the inner 'Krishna' or that inner power whose *swaroopa* is joy or bliss.

Q: What is inner voice and how does one recognise it?

Rajini: Inner voice is the voice of the Divine within us. We can call it as the voice of inner conscience, voice of the witnessing principle, or the manasakshi. If one decides to always follow the inner voice, in every aspect of life, one will soon reach the threshold from where Self-Realization will dawn by the Grace of God. In fact, one need not strive to study shastras, scriptures, Vedas, or even approach a Guru, visit a religious place or a shrine – if one always follows the inner voice. All that one requires is taken care of by the inner voice.

Q: How can we differentiate the inner voice from the voice biased by external factors?

Rajini: The inner voice can be influenced only through your attachments or *mamata*. When you are confused, simply step out of your shoes (body) and as a neutral judge ask yourself what should be done in a given situation. As a neutral person unconnected and unattached to the situation or circumstances, whatever comes forth is the pure inner voice! In this state, whatever your inner voice tells you will be in all honesty – the pure truth.

Q: Are other voices influenced due to our attachments not the voices of God? When and how does something become the inner voice?

Rajini: The answer to your first question is: Absolutely not!

They are not the voice of God. They are the voices of negative forces. As to your second question, let us put inner voice as an equation as under:

Inner voice = A-B+C-D

Now we will see what are A, B, C and D

A = The right values imbibed from your family, culture, tradition and society

B = Selfishness or attachment

C = Positive tendencies inherent in you in accordance with the rights and wrongs imbibed from your family, culture, tradition and society

D = Negative tendencies inherent in you that are not in accordance with rights and wrongs imbibed from your family, culture, tradition and society.

The effects of abiding by your inner voice are:
1. Helps thin down your mind
2. Reduces negative tendencies inherent in you
3. Increases positive tendencies in you

The real difficulty is not in not hearing the inner voice. Even a terrorist can hear it. However, the dense, negative tendencies inherent in someone make the inner voice less audible. That is all. But the real difficulty is in abiding with the inner voice at all times. It needs a tremendous amount of strength and courage to abide with the inner voice. It's definitely not a cakewalk; it's a tightrope walk, which further develops into walking along a razor's edge, before the mind becomes thin enough for Divine Grace to dawn upon one.

When a three or four-year old child tries to touch an item that it has been told not to touch, he will look at you from the corner of the eyes to make sure you are not watching him. That is because he knows that he is not supposed to do that. This information that he is not supposed 'to do that' is given by his inner voice. However, in spite of it, the outer voice compels him into doing it. Everyone, from a child to a hardcore terrorist, has this inner voice that tells him what is right or wrong.

Let us take another example. Suppose you are an employee in a company where one day you see the Manager misappropriating something from the office and accusing the cleaning boy for that deed, and then going to the extent of calling the police. Now, suppose you are the only person who has actually witnessed this act of misappropriation and you also have the evidence but out of fear of the repercussions its revelation would have on your job, you decide not to reveal the truth to the police. You make this choice not because you could not hear your inner voice, but because you were not willing to abide by the inner voice. Here an innocent person was being punished due to your instinct for self-survival as well. If you were ready to act truthfully with the attitude of 'come what may', you would have listened to and abided by your inner voice.

If, in the above example, the Manager is substituted by the cleaning boy, you would not have hesitated for a second to reveal what you saw him doing. This is because your self-interest here is not affected and it would not have any implications for you regarding your job. That is to say, the element of selfishness or attachment is the factor that influenced the inner voice, which later got so mixed up with the inner voice, and confused you into recognising which was the inner voice.

There is another aspect connected with the inner voice. Depending upon where you are born, the inner voice speaks differently. In a given set of situations the inner voice of an Indian, American and an African would show some differences because the education, family environment, traditions and cultures vary. If one finds it difficult to hear the inner voice, it is due to the negative tendencies, instincts, nature or vasanas which constitute one's mental makeup. The thinner the vasanas, the louder the inner voice. The denser the vasanas, the feebler the inner voice.

Simply follow the inner voice and live your life. Nothing more and nothing less is what anyone needs to do. Then all one has to do is wait and be amazed at what happens. Also remember that one's inner voice is the final judge, and no one can escape its judgements. One's inner voice is that tip of the Divine that one can feel and hold on to at all times. This alone can pull you fully into your Self, and that is what is called Self-Realization.

Q: If the inner voice gives different responses, which of these should be followed?

Rajini: You have an inner voice felt by you and that is yours alone, so follow that. You are confused because instead of going inwards and listening to your own inner voice, you are drifting outward and listening to other people's inner voices and the after-effects thereof. Do not do that. Do that which is always right as directed by your inner voice. You may hesitate to accept this advice probably because you are unaware of the course that nature takes. As long as one is unaware of the way natural forces work, and also fails to see that there are no lapses, one will not be able to always follow the inner voice. If you always follow your inner voice, natural forces will take care of everything and help you move steadily ahead in life.

Q: You earlier gave the example of a three-year old child who was told not to touch a particular object. However, his instinct compelled him to touch or hold it. That seems to be a more natural response than the external injunction of 'Don't touch that', doesn't it?

Rajini: The three-year old knows very well that he has to follow what he has been instructed to do. Yet, one child may abide by that as he has a natural instinct that is in accordance with what is right. Another child may not follow that instruction because he does not have such a strong natural tendency, and so he listens to what his mind, or outer voice, tells him to do. The difference is that one has to make an effort to do what is right. This effort too varies from person to person, and that effort is controlled by vasanas. When the mind knows that this person is going to listen only to his inner voice, it automatically becomes very thin over a period of time and the core becomes bigger. Eventually, a state is reached when the mind's interference ceases to exist and the inner voice at the core flows through the person unhindered – an unresisting flow of the natural forces.

Q: If the inner voice is in any way influenced, how can it be justified?

Rajini: It is here that your personal effort plays a big role. One has to put in a determined effort and that can be sometimes very tough indeed! That is why it is not for the weak-hearted. Only those who are strong and courageous will succeed in their efforts. It is only through this that the process of purification of the mind happens, and the mind becomes thinner and thinner. This process results in the maturity that comes with it. Divine Grace only dawns upon the one who is mature enough, and then he becomes Self-Realized.

Q: What about one's conditioning? When you are told not to touch something and you try to touch it, you may feel uncomfortable. If, on the other hand, you do touch it you feel guilty. But that 'I feel' is just conditioning. Would you feel uncomfortable or guilty if you were primarily not conditioned to feel so?

Rajini: Yes, I grant that everything is, as you have so rightly said, 'conditioned'. But the important thing is how to 'uncondition' or to use a better word, 'recondition'? The process indicated earlier will lead to 'reconditioning'. An unconditioned mind is one in which the sense organs function one hundred percent and the mind no longer interferes in the functioning of the sense organs, unless and until you decide to interfere using your mind. The process of abiding by one's inner voice thins the mind to the stage when God's Grace is showered upon a person and results in a 'no-mind' state.

A realized soul in a 'no-mind' state could be sitting with all the sense organs functioning with no interference from the mind. But if someone comes along and asks something, he will not sit like a vegetable or like a mentally challenged person. He will use his mind and reply if he feels he should answer. Here his mind is so much in control that it is just like his legs or arms that would not move without his permission. In a realized soul, you can find his eyes looking, ears hearing, nose smelling, and so on and so forth; but you will not find his mind interfering in the functioning of the sense organs. You will not find his mind defining, labelling and judging according to the workings of his sense organs. When his mind is fully in his control, it moves and functions only when required; otherwise the sense organs are left to function on their own without any unnecessary interference from the mind. This condition is known as being present in the Now.

Q: So we call the right voice as inner voice. Is the inner voice always right?

Rajini: Yes, you are right. Anything stuffed into the intellect is of any good only if it seeps down from the intellect to the heart and functions from there. May it seep down into your heart and start functioning there in your day-to-day living!

Q: I have read about the life and works of great people. Does the way of listening to my inner voice get affected by the knowledge I get from these books?

Rajini: The inner voice can be influenced by the kind of books you read. However, it can also be influenced by every righteous thought we imbibe from outside, whether it be through books or through observing righteousness in the lives of the people around us.

Q: How can one hear the inner voice?

Rajini: Who in the world has not ever heard the inner voice? Whenever you have been about to do something wrong, doesn't something inside stop you from doing it? It is another matter whether you abide by what you hear or not. Have you not heard this voice inside you? Yes, you have always heard it! Your inner voice always speaks to you; only you do not pay attention to it. Make that inner voice the guiding force by which to live your life. It is this light that will remove the darkness and reveal the truth. Accept it and do not judge the results. To accept things as they come requires a great deal of strength and courage. In any case you cannot escape what is coming to you irrespective of whether you cry and accept, or accept it with a proper understanding of the ways of nature.

Depending on your instinct, you might hear the inner voice feebly or loudly. Nevertheless, don't doubt the existence of your inner voice or the ability to hear it. As you were told earlier it's not the ability to hear that is the problem. Even in the case of terrorists, they hear their inner voice but they decide not to follow what they hear.

Try advising anyone, they will all clearly tell you that they know what is right and wrong but they nevertheless choose to do the wrong thing. Is not that the case? This is an inner journey. No one can ever see this journey. Every barrier is crossed in darkness. The more strongly you hold on to the inner voice, the more it will take care of you.

CHAPTER 3

How Can The Ego Be Diminished?

Practical Vedanta

Q: *What is Practical Vedanta?*

Rajini: Practical Vedanta is letting one's life flow on its own course, unhindered.

Q: *How do we let life flow on its own course?*

Rajini: First tell me, do you know 'who you are'? You are not the body, nor are you the mind. Is that right? Are you (the real you) the doer of anything, at anytime or anywhere? No! You, the real you, is not the doer. Now, the thoughts, words and actions seem to be arising from you as they arise from your body and mind – is that not right? The mind and the body are merely the instruments through which they flow. Whose is the flow? The flow is that of nature.

In Primary Science textbooks we are shown pictures of

nature depicting hills, mountains, birds, animals, rivers and so forth. How does everything in nature function? Look at everything in nature; it has its own flow. Everything has its own rhythm. We never see ourselves as part of nature as we are the ones learning and pointing to everything we see outside of ourselves as nature. In reality, this body and mind too is an integral part of nature. We never think of ourselves in that way. What we fail to understand is that the same natural forces control one's mind and this body too.

Think of a newborn baby. When he comes into the world, he sees his surroundings, feels the touch and the warmth of his mother. Then it is the world that he comes to know of first when he becomes aware of his sense organs. When he is hungry or wets his nappy, he feels uncomfortable and cries. On his needs being satisfied, he regains his comfort, stops crying and in the process feels the presence of his body. That is to say, the first things he comes to know of are the world, and then his body. He never comes to know his real 'Self'.

As he grows up, he observes that when he smiles he is hugged and loved, and when he wets his clothes he is admonished or scolded. When he shouts, cries and throws tantrums, he again experiences negative emotions from his parents. That which he feels as 'expanding' while he happens to do what is acceptable to his elders or parents, and that which he feels as 'shrinking' when he does what is not acceptable to them, he wrongly believes 'that something' to be himself. In reality, what is 'that something'? It was merely the response he received from his elders, and so he started believing the 'responses' to be himself.

All his life he is seen striving to make his illusory self or the ego – bigger and bigger. So he keeps avoiding that which 'shrinks' himself. Thus starts his folly! Ninety-nine percent of mankind struggles throughout life to make this illusory false sense of 'i' – bigger and bigger, and then die with that same illusion. This not only has a present but also has a past too in the forming of instincts and vasanas, which this very illusory 'i' also carried in the form of subtle vibrations in his mental sheath, from previous births. This striving or struggle is the real hindrance to what maybe termed the 'natural flow'.

On removal of the hindering factor, the inner voice alone remains and the unimpeded flow of the inner voice itself becomes the natural flow. What is left then is purely the flow of nature, the painless, blissful affair of life. All the pain in life is derived only out of hindrance and resistance to this flow. This is how one can let life flow unhindered on its own course.

Q: 'I am not the body' is comparatively easy to unserstand because the practice of meditation separates me from my body. But 'I am not the mind' seems more difficult because this 'endless ego' never ends. Will there ever be an end to this ego?

Rajini: Out of compassion alone a reply flows. It is only by living a righteous life that the process gets started and is set rolling towards the desired end. All the knowledge that you gather, all the *japa*, meditative techniques, *pranayama*, *pujas*; all the books that you read, all the satsangs that you take part in and so on; whatever you pursue has value only to the extent of helping you to live life righteously. Now, what effect does living a righteous life have on the whole process?

Living a righteous life leads to purification or thinning of the mind. Only a thin mind can be exhausted fully. Just like a speeding vehicle has to be slowed down before stopping, so also a dense or chaotic mind cannot be stopped all of a sudden, as it would create an imbalance and could overturn the mind in some cases. Now, if the mind is pure it would be at peace and less confused, as it knows what has to be done most of the time through its power of discrimination. It always remains enthusiastic, cheerful, energetic, and filled with positive thoughts.

So nature, out of sheer compassion for such a pure soul, creates circumstances in the form of people and situations where it tests one's purity. It has its own flawless laws without any loopholes, to bring blessings into your life. The quality of the blessings would depend on your vasanas and pending karma that have not yet reached you. This is where retaining the purity of your thoughts, words and actions would be essential. Even through the tough conditions that nature puts you in, if you hold on to your inner voice you will be moulded into God's beautiful instrument through whom He functions. This is like the hollow and empty flute (devoid of 'me', an egoless state) through which Sri Krishna creates musical notes hearing which all ardent seekers are drawn like a magnet.

If one passes through this phase of life successfully, one comes out as a mature soul. A sudden shift happens, everything changes at one point. The first vibration of the individual mind is the vibration of ego, and it is this absorption of the vibration of ego into the higher vibration of the Divine that leads to the egoless state or the 'no-mind' state. Here the one hundred percent purified mind, the 'no-mind', becomes stabilised. It no longer wavers, unless you decide to use it. This is that point which cannot be attained by mere human effort. All that is in man's hand is to reach that point and be available when, by His Grace alone, the shift happens.

CHAPTER 4

Why A Guru Is Necessary

Ignorance and the need for a Guide

Q: Why does one encounter confusion and contradictions along the spiritual path?

Rajini: Until the Truth is reached or revealed, there is ignorance all along the spiritual path. So it is bound to create confusion as all that has been learnt might, at different levels of ignorance, contradict one thing here and another thing there.

Imagine a pool with steps all around leading down to it. Think of what is above and around the pool as being the world, and the steps as the path leading to the Ultimate Truth – the pool of nectar. One way is to just dive into the pool from the top and realize that this is the true 'I'. The other way is to slowly, step by step, move down towards the Truth. When you go down one step, you cross one level of ignorance to hold onto another level of ignorance, which is of course a smaller one. This you are doing in the belief that you are bidding goodbye to a wrong notion, holding onto the Truth, whereas this is also at the ignorance level, which again has to be crossed by going further and further down the steps. At each step, you believe that the next step is the Truth, and leave the previous step. Every time you cross one step, you feel that you have learnt, understood, and removed so much ignorance to arrive at the Truth. But have you? Are you not still at the ignorance level, but with the belief that you have attained a great deal?

It is true that one learns a lot with every step taken, and that one crosses many hurdles. But it must be kept in mind that one is at different steps or levels, which are intermediaries at different stages of life. So it's natural to be confused, unless one is guided by an external Guru. One who can clearly see where exactly one is, what remains to be crossed in what aspects of life, in which aspects one has learnt a lot and in which one has learnt less is progressing on the path. Depending on the level one has reached and the strength of one's tendency to hold onto it, one has to be carefully guided to take each additional step and bring one as near as possible to the pool of nectar, or the essence of the Ultimate Truth. This is the most an external guide can do.

However, a tremendous amount of trust together with total submission of oneself to the external Guru or guide is a must. How else can one know that what was told to be the Truth in the previous step is now being revealed to be yet another level of ignorance, further indicating that the next step may reveal the Truth? The external Guru does this gently with much care and leads one to the brim of the pool. Do you see the beauty of it all?

Utmost faith is required, otherwise the possibility of leading a seeker to the pool is ruled out. What's more, the steps are crossed taking into consideration only the factors that have to be overcome in each individual case. Because of these reasons, it is easier to lead one who has not yet moved in that direction but who has reached maturity for the initiation, as compared to someone who has already started moving in the direction.

A final word: the plunge into the pool whether from the top, middle, or from the step nearest to the pool, can happen only by the Grace of God – the true Guru. The true Guru is the One inside you. The external Guru's role is only till you reach the brim. The level of purity that one has attained with sincere effort plays a big role. That is the factor that activates the true Guru with Divine Grace.

The need for an external Guru

Q: Is there a need for an external Guru? I have read two articles. One is titled 'Transcending the Need for a Living Guru' by Jiddu Krishnamurti. He says not to make him a Guru; he will not accept a disciple as the disciple destroys the Guru and the Guru destroys the disciple. In the second article, I came across a Sadguru who says that it takes a living Master to bring sutras alive. He says that when Patanjali wrote the Yoga Sutras he gave only threads. Can you please explain the contradiction in these two views?

Rajini: First let us ponder over what or who is a Guru.

The real Guru is not a person. It is a *tattva*. Activation of this Guru is the source of all knowledge. This real Guru who is internally within us, is essential for anyone to realize the Truth, or the Self! The external Guru can be a person and maybe classified under two broad categories. The first is the Guru whose internal Guru is activated, and the second is the one whose internal Guru is not yet activated. The external Guru whose inner Guru, or the real Guru, is activated maybe referred to as the Enlightened One. The other is a Teacher who teaches what he has learnt. When we refer to a Guru we are not talking of a Teacher. So, whom we are left with now is the Enlightened One.

To answer your question whether an external Guru is inevitable, my answer is a big 'No!' The external Guru has his limitations and at the most he can show you who is the real Guru. The real Guru can only get activated when the soul is sufficiently matured or 'ripened'. The external Guru's role is to take the seeker to that level of maturity where the real Guru gets activated: the real Guru's activation is the state of Enlightenment. It depends on our nature, or rather the purity of it, if we are a soul that needs a Guru or not. Depending on this, it is quite possible to reach that level of maturity without help from an external Guru. It then simply happens by Divine Grace.

For those whose basic nature is not all that pure, they will definitely require an external Guru to guide them on how to live righteously. Guidance from the external Guru will be effective depending upon the sincerity with which one follows the guidelines. Simply knowing them at an intellectual level will not take such persons any further. Here again, you see the limitation of the external Guru; his role is only to show the path to the real Guru. Once the real Guru is activated, the external Guru has no purposeful function and is acknowledged out of respect and gratitude, as he was instrumental in guiding one to the state in which one finds oneself now. It is this state of activation of the real Guru that Sri J. Krishnamurti is talking about when he mentions transcending the need for an external or living Guru.

In the second article, what is said as 'bringing sutras alive' refers to the role of the external Guru, where he guides the person who needs it on how to move ahead on the path consciously and righteously. Putting him on the right track, educating him on realities and truths, is what is meant here by putting life into spiritual practices.

Who can be an external Guru? He could be an enlightened person, or one who has studied the scriptures and shastras, or he could be a teacher. It could be a book, a dialogue simply overheard, an incident, or even Nature itself. Which of these will be the ideal external Guru would depend solely on the kind of soul one is, and one's own nature, vasanas and so on. Without a doubt, a living enlightened soul is the most powerful triggering factor as he guides with pin-pointed precision. Step by step, he removes ignorance and monitors the growth of the disciple.

If it were through books or recordings of the words of enlightened sages, they are undoubtedly much better than the books of non-enlightened ones. However, in the case of books, the drawback is the level for which they had been written. What has been written might not match with your level.

In a nutshell, both these articles have nothing contradicting each other and are, in fact, complementary to each other.

Faith in the Guru

I would like to elaborate on some matters here.

A simple method of realizing that there is only peace is by going into one's Self. But a person, who is unable to take that 'sudden plunge' into the pool, should take to other paths of arriving at the Truth.

A person who chooses the 'sudden plunge' method for Self-Realization or wants to live a peaceful life may start reaping its benefits. But until he attains it fully, he should not disclose to others what he is doing because it may attract unconstructive and unwarranted criticism. Indulging in conflicting arguments will only lead to further confusion between the two parties. They will keep arguing that their method is the only one or, perhaps, the better method towards the goal. But the moment both parties reach their final destination of Self-Realization, they will no longer have any arguments as they see no differences and also see that no 'one' method is better than the other. Whichever method one chooses would, if followed with sincerity and determination, ultimately lead to the desired result.

You may have seen that people go from one Guru

to another until they find the right Guru. The 'rightness' is actually not in the Guru or his method; it is in the suitability of the method to the person's nature. All Gurus are the same, whatever they may outwardly appear to be. And all methods can lead to the desired result. That is why it is often said that Gurus should not be judged; you can never know them until you yourself are 'realized', or until you find the very Guru who suits your nature.

An important factor is the trust and faith one has in the Guru. The Guru himself does not require it as he has nothing to gain, nor has he any desire except to help those who need it. He simply puts in sincere efforts with a pure heart expecting nothing in return. He simply rejoices in seeing a positive turn in the life of the seeker, whether it is through him or somebody else. The true Guru sees all, understands all; he has a clear vision of everything as he has attained realization of the Truth.

True Gurus come in different forms. Outwardly they may appear to be totally different, though inwardly they are all alike. Some may appear as typical Gurus who are strict and disciplined, while others may appear to come across as slightly unconventional or, perhaps, even half-mad. Others could come across as being rough, rude and short-tempered. Some observe silence, while others appear to be leading an ordinary life like anyone of us. Then there are others: those who appear to have renounced everything; those who indulge in religious ceremonies; those who believe in pomp and show; those who go to forests or the mountains and remain aloof from the world; those who function amidst the masses with great zeal and vigour.

Whatever they are outwardly, they are not that inwardly. Internally they are not attached to anything. They are compassionate towards everyone. If any harm is done to them, they never blame; they only bless. The Guru's blessings are powerful and are always there for all.

A true Guru can clearly gauge his disciple's level and requirements, and he accordingly takes steps for the benefit of his disciple in all sincerity and affection. It is because of this it is said that faith in the Guru is a very important element in the rise of the disciple towards attainment of his goal or to feel the desired change in his life.

CHAPTER 5

Why We Should Not Judge

Being Judgemental

Q: Why is there a need for these so-called modern day Gurus to propagate Hinduism? Hasn't it lasted for almost 5000 years without any propaganda?

Rajini: This question arises out of the conditioning of your mind. On what basis do you judge others if not on the basis of the conditioning to which your mind has been subjected? How valid are the opinions that you form or the judgements that you make?

You cannot judge others as long as you do not know the intentions behind their words and actions. God alone can judge; no one else can.

Understand the impossibility and insignificance of judging others. The only significant act a person can perform is to make an effort to be one hundred percent truthful and sincere in accordance with his own manasakshi, or the Divinity in him. This manasakshi, the inner voice or the inner conscience, is the only true judge. It registers everything exactly as it is and judges with all justice, in accordance with the laws of nature that have no loopholes or lapses.

So instead of criticising and judging others, concentrate on your inner world that comprises all your thoughts, words, and deeds.

Regarding the need for propagation of Hinduism, had the great Adi Sankara not come at the right time and all that happened through him not occurred, the treasure of Hindu philosophy and thought would probably have been lost for coming generations. If it is religion and not spirituality that you are talking about, it needs propaganda for survival. But if it is spirituality that you are referring to, then it does not need any kind of propaganda or promotion. Truth and spirituality have nothing to do with the preservation of any religion, scriptures or teachings. Religion is very much a state of the mind, while spirituality is beyond the mind.

On Fear

Q: I know that whatever is happening to me is destined to happen, and everything that is due to me will surely come. Then why am I anxious and filled with fear? How can I accept everything that comes in a positive way? How do I convince myself that I am neither the doer nor the enjoyer?

Rajini: Whatever the immediate cause of fear, every fear is ultimately the fear of the diminishing of ego. You only fear the diminishing of ego, and the greatest fear is the extinction of the ego. Look into it deeply. Whatever be the cause of fear, it has a tendency of making the ego feel small. Now you know ego is nothing but *aham-bhavam*. It is not *aham* but a *bhavam* only, something that is illusory or non-existent. What is the need for worrying or being anxious about the becoming small of something that is non-existent? What you really are is ever-existent. Nothing can make it less in any way; nothing can touch it. Then why worry and become anxious?

Now that you know that the real 'you' can never diminish, and also know that what you think is diminishing is something which is not really there, then what is this fear for? When you do not have any fears you will automatically not resist anything, and non-resistance is acceptance. What you resist persists in you as anxiety or negative thought-waves, which in all probability appear as manifested realities in your life. So if you fear, then in all probability you will be contributing by your present actions to materialise something that's negative, which you do not want. But when you welcome everything, or are ready to accept all that prakruti provides, you will not attract thoughts and events that are negative. Do you see the point behind this cause and effect?

When you are appreciated, you have the feeling of having grown bigger. You should know that it is only the ego that is growing bigger. When you are unappreciated, something inside becomes smaller, and that again is your ego. To ensure this does not happen you should, whenever you receive appreciation, directly confer that feeling to the

Divine with a bhawam, that all praise is Yours (God's), as You are the doer – not I. The same is true vice versa. When one does not own the credit of the good that comes, one will not own the bad either as it would have become a habit to give away everything to God. Thus one will not be touched by so-called negativities.

As long as you function within the mind you get the feeling that you are the doer, but when you go beyond the mind then you realize that everything that happens is a flow of nature. Moreover, if you look at the universe you know that everything in it is going on perfectly and it is not man who is controlling the universe. Therefore you will understand that man, who is even less than a worm in the entirety of the universe, is not the doer of his actions.

Dharma and Adharma

Q: *As part of my job, I have to arrange for the extermination of stray dogs by poisoning or shooting them. This causes me tremendous amount of pain as I love all animals and it makes me feel guilty of being the cause of their death. Can anything justify this killing of dogs to safeguard children, in the eyes of God?*

Rajini: It is the thought behind an act that makes it good or bad. The same act when done with wrong intentions becomes a bad act, but when it is done with good intentions and for a good purpose it becomes a good act. If a selfish motive drives one to do something, the act is rendered as Adharmic – that is against the law of Dharma. If it is done for the good of others, it becomes Dharmic. It's the intention that makes an act good or bad. This guideline should be followed in life when one exists in the illusory 'i'. It will lead one towards a purified state, and to that level of maturity when one is ripe enough to go beyond. This going beyond is a happening, and it happens by the Grace of God.

Now, to address the last part of your question: When a person goes beyond the mind, he no longer exists as one who is separate from all others. He is one with all. He simply exists and neither sees the body of the other, nor the body of any other being. He sees only the eternal Oneness, in which all forms of life – mankind and animals – are equal.

Loving the 'Self' vs. Selfishness

Q: I have heard you say that one must love the 'self' at all times. Is not 'loving the self' the same as 'selfishness'?

Rajini: Let me explain this to you by giving the following example:

Suppose X gives a vengeful blow to Y. In the process, not only is Y injured but so also is X. Now Y seeing the injury of X and the excruciating pain he is undergoing, gives first-aid to X. He consoles and takes care of X out of compassion. Seeing this, onlookers would remark on the selflessness of Y. But one can also look at it from a different viewpoint.

The act of Y can also be seen as an extremely selfish one, as you can see his selfish thought of not having done any wrong from his side. His thinking is that whatever X does is X's lookout, so why should he care what X does? He does not let that act of X influence his own acts and make them corrupt. Thus we can see that 'selfishness' and 'selflessness' are only words, and their real meaning is beyond these mere words.

Why did the act appear to be the most 'selfless' for one, and the most 'selfish' for the other?

The reason is the 'self' that each one sees is different. The one who sees all of it as a selfless act sees the 'self', which is in reality the ego. And the other who sees the whole act as a selfish one, sees the 'Self' that is the individual soul! So it is not so important if one is selfish or selfless. What is important is who is being selfish or selfless? If it is the ego you are thinking from, be selfless. If, on the other hand, it is the core or the individual soul you are thinking from, be selfish. Loving the 'Self' is to love the core and do what is good for the individual soul at all times. An act of selfishness caters to the needs of the ego and ignores the core or individual 'Self'. When you love your 'Self', or cater to what the core says, you are in effect living for others.

For catering to the soul or to the core, you need a healthy mind in a healthy body. The ideal way to achieve that is to identify those activities that do not cater to either of the two, and so discard such activities.

Acceptance

Q: After the demise of my father, my mother became very ill. My sugar level went up due to irregular food. I also suffered an injury to my left leg due to which I couldn't walk for some days. Generally, I am able to face events in a balanced manner. But this time it was much harder. Why?

Rajini: It is wonderful that you are able to face tough situations most of the time in a balanced manner. You can make it much easier on yourself by cultivating a healthy mind and a healthy body.

Try eating a cucumber, a carrot, a tomato, a guava, an orange or an apple every one-and-a-half hour or two hours. It is easy to carry and easy to eat too. At home, you can have the option of oats. It would be a good investment in your health. In this way, you can manage your nutrition and can work towards good health even during hard times. Eating raw vegetables and fruits has a positive effect on the mind as they help remove toxins accumulated while undergoing difficult times or periods of stress.

You should learn to accept things as they are, and as they come. How we handle and cope with situations makes all the difference. Acceptance is inevitable. Whether you cry and accept, or you internally remain calm and accept, one way or the other you have to accept. How you accept situations not only influences the present, but also influences the future. Watch your thoughts, words, and deeds under all circumstances, and ensure that they are in accordance with your inner voice, the Divine in you. This will prevent negative feelings from arising when you are faced with adverse situations. This will help in the process of diminishing the illusory 'i' or aham-bhavam.

You should accept the so-called problems that arise as being blessings in disguise. The tougher the situation, the more the alertness, strength and courage one has to gather to act righteously and live according to one's inner voice.

Here are two other things you can do that will help you act wisely in any situation:

1. Sit silently for some time. Don't think of anything. You may do this as and when you find the time, but try to do it as the first thing in the morning when you wake up, and also as the last thing before you go to sleep.

2. When you feel totally confused, go to a place where you will not be disturbed. Sit straight with folded legs, close your eyes, and keep your mind blank.

Divine Grace will be showered upon you.

CHAPTER 6

Karma, Vikarma, Akarma

Q: Would you please tell me the difference between Karma, Vikarma, Akarma, and give some examples?

Rajini: Karma is your 'righteous action' and action includes both its doing and not doing.

Vikarma is 'unrighteous action' and this too includes both its doing and not doing.

Akarma is righteous action done without the sense of doership.

When we say 'action,' it does not mean just the mechanical act of doing or not doing; it is also inclusive of thoughts, words, and deeds.

Karma

Here are some examples: If a child falls and you help him get up and console him so he stops crying, your act is righteous. If a poor boy who stole a piece of bread is being beaten up in public for stealing but you abstain from participating in the beating, your 'inaction' amounts to righteousness. You may say all acts done or not done by you after listening to your inner voice or conscience amount to karma.

Vikarma

Any act done or not done, that is against your inner voice, will amount to Vikarma. For instance, if you behave rudely with someone just because you are tense or in a bad mood, or let out your anger on an innocent child, or in your heart of hearts even think of doing harm to someone, all these thoughts or actions will amount to Vikarma.

Akarma

This is not a state that is achievable by all. No doubt it would happen to everyone at some point of time, and that point of time is when one transcends and goes beyond the mind. This state occurs only by Grace of the Divine. Let's explain this in a simpler way:

Akarma is righteous action done or not done without the sense of doership, which is also known as *Karthruthwa Bhodam*.

The 'Doing' state of Akarma

This means that while the 'doing' is going on there is no mental activity, unlike the mental activity that goes on in persons who have not yet transcended the mind. One may appear to be busy doing this or that, while mentally nothing is being done as the mind is in a state of total stillness. One will use the mind only to the extent to which it is required for that particular work, and where even that is not required, like in routine mechanical work, one is totally centered in stillness. In both cases, no sense of being the 'doer' is present.

The 'Non-Doing' state of Akarma

This means that while the 'non-doing' is seen outwardly when one is simply sitting doing nothing, one who has transcended the mind is in reality not doing 'nothing'. This is because one is totally centered in the total expanse of nothingness or stillness. The powerful vibrations of such a mind radiate a tremendous amount of positivity that expands and embraces the entire universe.

Akarma happens by the Grace of the Divine. And when does Divine Grace dawn? It occurs when one is ripe and mature. Ripeness happens when one's mind is pure. Thus, doing one's karma and abstaining from Vikarma are powerful tools for purifying the mind.

Actions of an Enlightened Being

First let us look into who is an enlightened being. If *Shiva* is the God tattva and *Shakti* its powers, then the enlightened being is one who has merged both Shiva and Shakti within him.

Whatever is seen as having been done by such a being is not actually done by him. He is hollow, absolute nothingness. Only Divinity that has turned the being into a perfect instrument in the hands of the Almighty, through which the enlightened being acts, does it. In short, an enlightened being can be seen doing many things whereas in reality there is nothing he has to do, nor is he doing anything. This is the truth.

Now what does such an individual do?

Enlightened beings see beyond. They see that things are happening in the way they are destined to happen according to the laws of nature and Divine Will. If natural forces decide to use such a being as an instrument, then although your eyes would see that something is being done by him, in reality he is not doing anything.

Such a being may also at times decide to demonstrate the path for attainment so that it becomes easier for others to follow. Another such being could be seen sitting in one place with eyes closed, without the slightest movement of his body for a long period of time. People feel he is not doing anything in the physical, worldly sense, but he is doing so much. This the worldly eyes cannot see. The very presence of these enlightened beings is a blessing for all.

Dharma and Swadharma

Now let's find out what is 'my' Dharma or *Swadharma*. But first, let's find out whose Dharma or Swadharma? Only after finding the answer to this question should we proceed further.

When one realizes who is this 'i', then one has nothing to do – neither Dharma nor Swadharma – because nature or natural forces do everything. Then to whom are the concepts of Dharma and Swadharma applicable? They are applicable to the illusory 'i' i.e. the ego or aham-bhavam. They are applicable to the one who is shrouded in the veil of ignorance.

Dharma is a set of rules or guidelines that help you to realize your true 'Self'. The reason for finding yourself as the illusory 'self' in an illusory world is your being bound by the laws of causation, or Karmic laws. You are born in this world as a result of past karma. While you are here, you undergo a lot of *dukha* i.e. sorrow. These sorrows are due to your Adharmic acts in past lives. Therefore, the shastras or scriptures give you guidelines to clear your past negative actions so that you don't end up creating further negative karma. The shastras lay down several 'Do's and Don'ts' like practicing non-violence, truthfulness, avoidance of greed, lust, desires, anger, jealousy, and so on.

How do these guidelines help you grow out of the sorrows you experience in this world?

It is only Adharmic actions that lead to a situation like this. If we experience any happiness or pleasure, again it is the result of our past Dharmic deeds. In light of this knowledge, there are guidelines given in shastras for doing good deeds. These guidelines are to be fully complied with in thoughts, words and actions if *sukha* or pleasure is to be increased, and dukha or pain reduced. It is at this stage that the question of what is Dharma and Swadharma arises. The norms and guidelines laid down in the shastras are true at all times. They do not change with time. Being truthful is one of them.

Being Truthful

This means complying with the Ultimate Truth at all times. It is the only Truth and it never changes with time. So, always remember and be aware that you are *Atma tattva* and that God resides in the hearts of all. This consciousness will naturally give you all the qualities that are good, and any act of yours arising from this state of consciousness would be nothing but Dharmic.

A natural consequence of doing everything in this state of consciousness would be:

1. You will automatically stop thinking from the centre of your false 'I' and start thinking from the centre of the true 'I'.

2. You will automatically start seeing yourself in everything else, as God that resides in you also resides in everything else.

Now, can Dharma and Swadharma be different from each other? 'Swa' means 'Self' and 'Dharma of Self' – the real 'I' – is 'Swadharma'. Dharma also essentially means the same.

Swadharma is specifically used only to highlight the real 'I' hidden in Dharma. Its purpose is only to make you realize that Dharma is not that of the body. Dharma of the body is essentially *Paradharma*.

Thus, Swadharma and Dharma essentially mean abiding completely in Self-consciousness.

Predestination and Free Will

Q: If everything is predestined then what is the role of personal effort? I fail to understand the meaning in trying for something, if everything is predestined.

Rajini: Before I answer your question, it is essential for you to understand that there exists only the unchanging and the eternal, whatsoever name you want to give it. The moment you start speaking about the Truth, at that very instant, the Truth is rendered into falsehood. Thus it has to be very clearly understood that whatever is spoken of here, pertains to falsehood or that which is illusory. Since whatever is spoken of here is at the level of ignorance, this has to be kept in mind all throughout while reading this.

According to our ancient seers everything is predestined. Not a leaf will move without God's Will. We are nothing but tools in His hands. There is a saying in Hindi, *'Daane daane pe likha hai, Khaane waale ka naam'.* This means that 'On each and every grain is written the name of the person who is going to eat it'. There is also a beautiful saying in Zen: 'The snow falls, each flake in its appropriate place'.

What then is the meaning in trying for something if everything is predestined?

It is quite likely that a logical mind will question the role of personal effort. One obviously would say that each one of us has two options open in front of us, in everything we do.

For example, when I buy a shirt, if I choose the grey one, I will be the owner of that. If I choose the brown, then I will have that. So I can choose to exercise my free will. Then how do you say everything is predestined when free will is experienced by me in every little thing that I do? It is definitely my choice if I want to drink coffee or tea.

Whether everything is predestined or everything is as per our free will, it is only after clearly understanding this aspect that we can proceed further.

Let us look at the statement: 'Whatever happens now, at this moment, is 100% predestined'.

Let us understand what this really means. But first we must know how nature functions. Everything that happens is the effect of a cause. This maybe termed as 'the law of cause and effect' or 'the law of karma'. This means that our own actions bear fruit, or that all fruits are the result of actions that have already been performed. Thus, for a result to happen there has to be some act or karma that has already been done, and something that has already been done can no longer be changed. This virtually makes the result or consequence of that action a predestined one, or we may say that whatever happened was destined to happen in that way only.

It's like an arrow that's been shot out of a bow. Here the arrow is karma, which includes thoughts, words, and deeds. The bow is the individual. An arrow that has been shot is already destined to pierce a certain point of a target, at a certain time. Once the arrow has been released from the bow, the time and place of its piercing is already decided. It only requires the distance to be travelled and a certain time in the process to elapse. The piercing of the arrow at a particular place and at a particular time is the fruit of the happenings that we see around us. If it is clear what it means when we say 'what happens now is completely predestined', then we can understand how everything is predestined. By 'everything' one means everything that has ever happened, and everything that will ever happen.

Now let us address the confusion one would have that if everything in the future too is predestined, then what's the need for putting in any effort?

Let's again take that very statement: 'Whatever happens now, at this moment, is 100% predestined'.

Now can anything happen anytime other than at this moment? No, nothing can happen at any moment other than 'Now'.

Can anything happen in the past? No, nothing can happen in the past. Think logically: how can anything happen in the past? Does anyone say this is happening in the past? Or, can anyone say that somebody is sneezing in the past, or the dog is barking in the past? Likewise, can anything be happening in the future? Can you say X is sneezing in the future or the dog is barking in the future?

Therefore, we can conclude that all that has ever happened has always happened in the Now.

Thus these two statements when put together clearly prove that everything is predestined:

1. Whatever happens Now, at this moment, is 100% predestined.

2. All that has ever happened has always happened only in the Now.

Now, there is another thing that has to be clearly understood. If it is the actions of the past that create all happenings in the present, then all actions done by you now would create results in the future. This is where you have free will. You have the free will to choose between the good and bad, Dharma and Adharma, righteous and unrighteous. Depending on what you choose to do, you will reap the result. Thus, although whatever happens at all times is predestined, by using your free will you can definitely mould your future.

While this answers your immediate question, I am taking the liberty of stretching this a little further in order to give it completeness.

Ponder over who has the free will or who is subject to predestiny. Free will or predestiny is for the illusory 'i' and the realization of the real 'I' takes you beyond both. Then there is neither free will nor is there anything that's predestined. Absence of both is the real state.

The Bhagavad Gita

Q: Why did Lord Krishna teach the Gita to Arjuna, and not to Duryodhana? That would have avoided the war and there would have been no killing.

Rajini: Krishna is the innermost core of us – the Atma tattva! Arjuna is the egotistic personality. The Divine element in us gets activated only when the ego surrenders completely.

Only when Arjuna lays down his weapon, the Gandhiva, and goes down on his knees does he realize the Ultimate Truth. It is only after the realization that all that his ego has learnt, studied, acquired and achieved is in fact of no use to him, does he surrender to the Divine. And only when this total surrendering happens does the Divine start flowing through the hollow and empty instrument of the body, which is devoid of the ego. When the ego surrendered in Arjuna, the 'Inner Divinity' in him became activated and the Divine music of the Bhagavad Gita began to flow.

CHAPTER 7

Philosophy And Reality

Theism vs. Atheism

Q: A theist believes in the existence of God. On the other hand, an atheist has nothing to do with the soul, rebirth or God. Will an atheist who serves mankind selflessly with devotion, attain salvation?

Rajini: Why not! He will attain salvation and probably attain it faster than a theist who might, in the process of believing and reaffirming his beliefs, get diverted from the path. For example: If one were to tell a theist that there is no such thing as God and it's all a figment of his imagination, will he be able to tolerate this? The real test is here. If one is not able to love and accept his fellow beings by seeing the Divine in them, and instead feels hatred for them, that hate too has been inculcated by vested interests in the name of God!

You have made a statement saying, 'serves mankind with devotion'. Is that not the very purpose for which the existence of all gods is designed? You have mentioned 'devotion'. What is that? Is that not the highest order of prayer you can offer to God, and is mankind not a manifested form of the Divine?

You have also used the phrase 'being selfless'. What else does it mean if not immortal soul, pure consciousness, the real 'Self'? The second category that you mention, that of the atheist, is the firmer, truer devotee of God. These are only words and it makes no difference whether you refer to them as atheists or something else. Therefore, it is not the term 'theist' or 'atheist' that is important. What matters is what the person is like inside, what his bhavam is, how compassionate he is towards all beings.

Advaita and Mithya

Q: Why do Advaitins want to teach the theory of Advaita to the world, while this theory itself states that the world is illusory, and a person himself is Brahman?

Rajini: A realized Advaitin never teaches Advaita theory to the world. He may at the most speak a few words sometimes to help clear some doubts that may arise in a genuine seeker.

Q: The Advaitin only knows that Brahman exists, that he himself is that Brahman and that the world is mithya. This being his belief, and having crossed all illusions, why does he still want to teach this theory to illusory characters in an illusory world?

Rajini: Mithya means that everything is an illusion that keeps changing all the time and so it can never be captured. If you look at things from the micro level, nothing remains as it is even for a split second. Your body might appear to be present for so many years, but are you the same body that was born some years back? No, it does not have even a single cell that it was born with yet you feel that you are the same, but the reality is not that. A right understanding of mithya would clarify your doubts.

Q: My question is to any realized Advaitin. I think Shankaracharya wrote all his wonderful bhashyas, granthas after he realized himself to be Brahman and the world as illusory. What then was the need to write those and impart that 'understanding' to his shishyas who also were illusions? Did he still see an illusory world after his Realization?

Rajini: Firstly, how do you know he wrote it all after he became Realized? Secondly, a Realized person would at all times communicate the right knowledge, at the right time, to the right seeker, in the required manner for resolving and removing all the knots in a seeker of the truth. The removal of these knots helps the seeker to continue progressing on the path up to that point where the Grace of the Divine – the happening of Realization – dawns upon him.

Q: One who comes out from a dream cannot see dream characters after that nor can he communicate with them. One who is in a dream cannot say he is dreaming. In which state are the Advaitins?

Rajini: The example of dreams is given only for a comparative understanding. Unlike in the dream state, you do realize fully well that this world is mithya at the very moment Realization happens. But you will still have the ability to be very much in the illusory world, and keep interacting with it as though a play is being enacted. You are not shaken as before because now you know, and this knowing of the '*mithyatva* of the world' is different not just intellectually, but deep within your being.

Q: So does this mean that Advaitins, who shared or tried to share their knowledge through their works, were not all Realized and that we can't rely on their works?

Rajini: Advaitins shared their knowledge with true seekers and they have always benefited. One begins to rely on their works only when one is ready or matured enough to accept and believe in what is shared by them. Until then, doubt prevails and one keeps questioning the validity of their knowledge.

Q: Change doesn't mean mithya for me. Mithya for me is something that is not present at all but appears to be present; change is that which happens in something that really exists. If something is changing, then that means it should exist forever in one form or the other, doesn't it?

Rajini: If you prefer using some other word instead of mithya since it conveys a conflicting meaning to you, that is fine so long as you have the right understanding of it. If you look at 'change' in a deeper sense, it will take you to that what you understand by the word 'mithya'. But for understanding such subtle aspects one has to have a very clear intelligence, and for a very clear intelligence one has to have a pure mind with not many vibrations in it. And for a pure mind, one has to purify his vasanas or instincts, and for the vasanas to become pure one has to do sadhana.

Q: Since we don't know whether Adi Shankara was Realized or not while he was writing his works, we cannot then take them as truths. According to me, whoever can satisfy my logical enquiry with their interpretation of Shruti is a Realized One. Wouldn't you agree?

Rajini: No amount of proof even by the Realized person himself will convince you of his Realized state. This can only be felt by matured souls and other Realized persons. Even if a Realized person tells you that he is not Realized, the Realized state of the soul will be felt with a tremendous impact by a matured soul, and beyond all doubt by another Realized soul. One has to wait for the right time and no conviction is required for knowing what your conscience tells you. Live accordingly, that's all.

Q: If mithya means unreal, and the changing principle is also false – then the knowledge you receive from any source is also mithya because all knowledge has its source in mithya. Do you agree with what I am saying?

Rajini: You have a fine mind and a courageous spirit for having spoken so openly about these hard to accept truths. You are absolutely right in what you say. Such teachings are not imparted to everyone; they are revealed in total secrecy by a Realized soul to only a very mature seeker. Although you possess a sharp intelligence, you have yet to grow more mature so you can understand the deeper aspects of what you are asking. However, I will say a few words to you.

All knowledge is mithya as you say. But that is only relatively correct. However, don't underestimate the relative truth in it. If you ignore the relative truth realizing the absence of absolute truth in all knowledge, it is likely that you may lose your head after entering the spiritual realm.

It's like a staircase and you have to realize the mithyatva at every step, see the truth in the next, and keep climbing until you reach the top. One has to drop everything before that transition and the crossing happens. Everything happens by Divine Grace and then transformation occurs.

Q: Your argument is that the very concept of mithya in itself is mithya because the concept itself has the same source. What I am saying is when you think 'all this world is an illusion', then that very thought itself should be mithya. In other words, this means that the mithya idea of 'world is an illusion' cannot prove the world's mithyatva and so the whole theory collapses, doesn't it?

Rajini: You are absolutely right! You have asked that why do we want to try to negate the existence of changing entities after we know it is illogical to do so. In answer, I have this to say: It happens only when nature or prakruti itself starts the process on its own.

The moment Realization happens, there is only Realization, no 'Realized One' remains! There is neither the subject nor the object. Just the Being.

Philosophy is Scientific, but it is not a Science

Q: Philosophy generates ideas, which then need to be put to scientific scrutiny before they are accepted. Science is a process that follows evidence. If some of these ideas are accepted without evidence, or despite evidence to the contrary, then that philosophy has degenerated into spiritualism or religion. Then aren't both dealing in falsehood?

Rajini: One should not make sweeping generalisations. It is fairly easy to get evidence for whatever spirituality or philosophy says. All you have to do is conduct a simple experiment: stop all thoughts, even the thought that you need to stop all thoughts, for a while and remain silent for as long as you possibly can. Then experience for yourself the ultimate of all philosophies. After that, come back here with all the philosophies that you have discovered.

Q: For evidence to be scientific, wouldn't it be better if it is accepted only after several scientists have tested and verified it individually?

Rajini: Here too, any number of them could do the experiment repeatedly and confirm the evidence for themselves. Did you try this out? Do it first and come back with the results of the experiment. I tell you, all your confusions will dissolve forever if you succeed in the experiment.

The Vedantas are endorsements for the results that you get from the experiment. Not only the Vedantas, but also the results of all those having experienced that state can be considered as proof.

Advaita and Dvaita

Q: Can a true student of Advaita continue as a believer in gods? After reading some Advaitic texts can he again offer flowers, or perform yagna with the same passion as he did earlier? Will he not feel it's pointless even though he may not have actually reached the Advaitic state as yet?

Rajini: It is not essential for anyone to offer flowers or do yagna in the first place, let alone a follower of Advaita.

Those who have a tendency towards such rituals only do it, and a follower of Advaita who has such instincts will not have any difficulty in continuing with his practice. If a student of Advaita has an enlightened person as his Guru, and if he has full faith in him, then that person will be seen doing all the pujas with all the required passion and compassion.

This happens either due to the right understanding of Advaita in totality, or due to the trust in his Guru. He will continue doing the rituals until they get dropped of their own accord, or until his Guru instructs him to stop doing them when he feels it is the right time to do so.

Why do we need God?

One may as well ask, 'Why food?' It's only for the hungry who need it! 'Why medicine?' Again, it's only for the sick who need it! The value of anything is only for the one who needs it.

Until the grace of nature dawns upon him, a person exists only in his body consciousness. For him, life is meant only to fulfill the body's needs. When he evolves to the next stage, then nature creates those circumstances wherein he is compelled to see beyond the needs of the physical body. This brings him to that awareness when he starts performing good karma. The next level of evolvement is when he stops doing good just to satisfy his own needs, and starts doing good at all times for the benefit of others.

The point to be understood is that whatever stage one is in, one will have only that level of understanding. One has to pass all such stages to reach the state of Realization.

Now, the need for God increases and His meaning changes as one evolves. So the one who needs Him gets whatever it is that will be of great benefit to him. Will he then not sing the praises of that?

Therefore, understand that everything is a tool and using these tools one goes beyond, and then they are of no use to you. Because then one realizes that everything was a stepping-stone towards the goal, and stepping-stones that were so tremendously powerful then may continue to retain their utility, or they could be discarded. Both decisions would be right. Many a time, such tools are retained so they can be given to others who are following the person who has benefited from their use. This is done out of sheer compassion for others so they are not misled on their journey.

CHAPTER 8

Practical Considerations For A Seeker

Practicality of Vedanta

Q: If a student wants to do well in his studies, a graduate wants a good job, a bachelor wants a wife who can understand him, a man wants financial stability for himself and his family – can Vedanta help him?

Rajini: Vedanta means the end of the Vedas and that would mean that one who has studied all of them would have, in all probability, achieved the Self-Realized state.

What you mean by Vedanta, I think, is an aspirant studying the Vedas, practicing the teachings they contain, and desirous of the results you have mentioned thereof. If you are practicing the teachings correctly, then whatever you are seen to be doing would be best for you in the given circumstances. All your questions are actually pointing towards getting results, but you should shift your focus from the results to your thoughts, words, actions, and deeds. Good results will inevitably follow right actions.

When Learning becomes a Hindrance

Q: Why does spiritual learning become a hindrance at times in progressing further on the path to Self-Realization?

Rajini: This can happen because of the following reasons:

1. Learning by reading the scriptures is an intellectual process and misinterpretation of the texts could occur causing a hindrance. The process of Self-Realization begins only if there is initiation by a Guru or a Realized person.

2. There are people who have systematically learnt the scriptures, have a complete understanding of them, and who are also capable of speaking with great clarity on the subject. But the very fact of their superior knowledge and abilities gives a tremendous boost to their ego. In such a case, learning will become a hindrance for their true development in the direction of Self-Realization.

3. Another reason could be that an aspirant, having learnt everything there is to learn, has developed a strong desire to attain the state of liberation. Here, the very desire proves to be a hindrance in the attainment as desire stems from the ego. As long as there is ego, or as long as there are desires, there cannot be true liberation.

4. Consider someone with a great deal of learning but an incomplete understanding of the teachings.

This would naturally result in tremendous confusion and be the source of hindrance. Even if one has acquired right understanding through the proximity of a Sadguru but practices nothing in his life, this cannot lead to any further progress in the spiritual path. All progress on the spiritual path starts only when things learnt are reflected in one's life.

Seeping into the Heart is Vital

In spiritual matters a clear intellectual understanding is the first step. This starts showing results only after the understanding flows from the intellect down to the heart, which is where it is put into practice. Ideas that remain only at the level of the intellect are like seeds stored safely in an airtight container, waiting for suitable conditions in which they can germinate, grow and mature to ripeness.

When we say, 'a clear understanding is the first step', does it mean it is an inevitable step in the process without which nothing can happen? The answer is 'No'. Do trees and animals go about finding how to live and what to follow? They do not, because they have that knowledge within them and it flows out naturally. The shoots of a plant automatically turn towards sunlight. The plant doesn't need an outside source to tell how to start the process of photosynthesis. Similarly, all the information we will ever need is within us. Depending on situations and circumstances, it will be revealed.

So there is no need to turn your head outwards and

search for theoretical answers. Your inner consciousness always guides you according to your circumstances and situation. All you have to do is follow that intelligence. Then growth and maturity becomes effortless.

Iruthoni

Q: You told me something about 'Iruthoni' or two boats. Can you explain it clearly and tell how it can affect me adversely?

Rajini: The two boats are:
1. The 'within the mind' state; and,
2. The 'beyond the mind' state.

If you keep each of your legs in two separate boats you will surely fall into the water. You told me that you don't want to dive deep into the beyond in one plunge, and that you only want to move step by step. In the former instance, one moves out of ignorance in one go and stabilises there.

However, the path chosen by you is to be in the vast sea of ignorance from where you can move slowly, leaving behind one level of ignorance after another. You are now in the 'within the mind' state. Don't mix the state of 'beyond the mind' into your life now. Whatever information you may have collected about the 'beyond the mind' state should not be implemented with the norms you have to follow in the 'within the mind' state.

For instance, you know that you have to do good at

all times. At the same time, you have the information of 'beyond the mind' state that nothing is good or bad. If you try to mix up both, you will fall down. It is equivalent to putting each foot into two separate boats and will lead to disaster.

Moving beyond Dukha

Q: Does undergoing dukha lead to Self-Realization?

Rajini: It is the way and attitude with which dukha is handled that makes all the difference. Whatever maybe the gravity of dukha being experienced, whatever maybe its cause, one has to follow one's inner voice so that one thinks, speaks and acts through one's manasakshi, however difficult it maybe to follow one's conscience.

If one puts in sincere effort following his inner voice, the rest follows automatically and leads to Self-Realization by Grace of the Divine.

Margas or Paths

Q: There are so many margas like bhakti, jnana, karma and yoga. Which marga is superior and which one should I follow?

Rajini: In bhakti marga you either have bhakti, which is devotion or love for the Divine, or you pray to God. Bhakti is the highest form of love involving total surrender to the Divine. When there is total surrender, the entity called 'you' is no longer there. Then that which is working through you is the Divine. When the one called 'you' is fully subjugated or diminished and the Divine alone exists, the body then exists as an instrument of God. The illusory 'i' is gone. The highest prayer one can perform is thinking good, speaking good, and doing good with all sincerity and truthfulness, and seeing God in all by maintaining and attaining the highest level of purity in the heart. In other words, attaining a state of selflessness.

In jnana marga, through knowing the truths you realize who you really are and understand its nature. In the process you discard what you thought you were i.e. the illusory 'i'.

In karma marga, you do your Dharma without the feeling of doership attached to it, and you do not have any desire to reap the fruits of it either. When you do good deeds in this manner, the sense of 'you' as well as your desires vanish in the process. Here too, the illusory 'i' disappears.

In yoga marga, you try to control the mind through controlling your breath. Controlling the breath will help in controlling the mind and its activities:

Mind → illusory 'i' → Mine (attachment) → Desires (wanting things to be mine) → Actions (for the fulfillment of desires) → Anger due to unfulfilled desires → Intellect gets contaminated (*buddhi nasham*) → Destroys peace.

All your efforts should be directed to break this chain at the place where you think it is necessary to break it, so that the damage is minimised. Either you try to acquire control over your anger, or try to ensure there are no actions done that stem from desire or any selfish motive. No desire means no anger. When you go beyond anger you give up attachment. When you are not attached to anything, you are not affected by the coming and going of anything in your life. When the presence or absence of anything doesn't make any difference to you, how can you have a desire for it? When you either directly or through the path of jnana, karma, bhakti or yoga strike at the illusory 'i' and perceive the true 'I', everything down the chain is shattered. It is at this state of Self-Realization that you happen to go beyond the mind. The mind has then been conquered.

All these are not independent paths; they are interwoven. There can't be a karma marga without bhakti and jnana. There can't be a jnana marga without karma and bhakti. There can't be a bhakti marga without jnana and karma. There can't be a yoga marga without karma, which includes jnana and bhakti. You may start with any of the margas, but as you progress further on the path, all other margas have to join hands for its completion. No marga can by itself lead you to the ultimate goal of Self-Realization. Along the way, one by one, all the streams will join to reach the ocean.

Now to address your question regarding which marga is suitable for you. One thing about you is, and many have this problem, that there is a great deal of clutter in your mind. People who have never gone into this field to find out what is there do not have this problem. So it's easier for them to follow directions when they find the right guide. The one who has gone into it in some depth often feels that he needs the help of a true Guru.

The first important step is the removal of the clutter.

In your case, the jnana marga is the only one that can effectively remove the clutter of misinformation that has been misleading you. However, all methods ultimately lead to the same result. Sincere efforts have to be made to reach the final goal until you come to abide in that state by Grace of the Divine.

Thoughtless Gaps between Two Thoughts

Q: Recently, I have begun to follow Nisargadatta Maharaj's recommended 'I AM' meditation path. However, according to my understanding, it's not the path that we choose but the intensity with which we follow it that brings the desired results. Isn't that so?

Rajini: Whichever path you are following is perfectly fine. Are you able to sit in a thoughtless state and, if so, for how long? It is these thoughtless gaps that you have to stretch longer. Further, use your mind only when it is required and only to the extent it is required. This using of the mind should be one hundred percent in accordance with your manasakshi or conscience. Do everything in this manner and accept whatever comes without discrimination. Nothing more and nothing less is required.

Q: I am not sure if I can stay in the 'no-mind' state. When I am alone and with nature I feel comfortable and love oozes out towards the trees, birds, cats etc. I don't really understand what you mean when you say extend the thoughtless state.

Do you think I have to change anything or just continue with the practice?

Rajini: What you have described is exactly what should be happening, and this should be happening at all times. Try to extend the 'no-mind' state, which in effect means that you are in a thoughtless state. Accept everything that is without discriminating. Try to stay in the present moment, the Now. By Grace of the Divine, you will enter the 'no-mind' state in a natural way, effortlessly! Whatever practices you are doing, understand that they are only for helping you live in a righteous manner. Continue with that.

CHAPTER 9

Secrets Of Gayatri Mantra And Athatho Of Brahma Sutras

Athatho

Q: What does 'Athatho' in Brahma Sutras imply?

Rajini: Athatho in Brahma Sutras is the stage a person reaches on maturity when he realizes that all the knowledge that he has learnt, all the virtues that he has imbibed, all the meritorious acts that he has done, all the *punya* that he has earned, all the purity that has been attained – are of no use at all. They are of no use because he finds himself in a position where all that he has earned is incapable of rendering any help in the situation he is in. He is unable to find a right solution and nothing helps him. He finds himself in a totally helpless situation.

It is at this point that he gives up everything: all the so called good, the ego, all that he does, because nothing works, nothing helps. It is only at this juncture that total surrender to the Supreme happens. It is now (Athatho) that the Supreme takes over and reveals all (Brahman).

Brihadaranyaka Upanishad – a Doubt

Q: What does this line from Brihadaranyaka Upanishad mean: 'Where there is separateness, one sees another, smells another, tastes another, speaks to another, hears another, touches another, knows another, but there is a unity, without a second, that is the world of Brahman'?

Rajini: This means that just as the two hands of a person would, but for his consciousness, never know they actually belong, similarly, it is only after 'i' realize that 'i' am that true 'I' or the 'Brahman' that I come to know the oneness or unity without a second.

It is only the shift from unconsciousness to consciousness that brings the knowing that the two hands are mine, they constitute me, and are not separate. In the same way, the shift into the state of Brahman or the real 'I' from the ego self or the illusory 'i' or the small 'i' brings in the knowing of the oneness of all, and that there is no second. Only 'I' alone is! It needs the consciousness of a person to know the oneness of the two hands. Likewise it needs the awareness as Brahman or existence in the true 'I'. In this oneness there is unity with no second and no separateness.

When you are asleep, the real knowing of your hands is not there but intellectually you know, that is all. Real knowing is there only when you are awake. Isn't that true? In the same way, you can intellectually understand this Oneness in the state of Brahman. But for a real knowing of the state of Brahman it must happen, or an awakening is essential.

Sleep is a state that has to happen of its own accord. You cannot go to sleep the moment you wish to, nor can you awaken yourself from sleep unless it happens. In the same way, this Big Sleep is a happening and the True Awakening too is a happening. Just as a sleeping man would either be awakened on his own at the saturation point of sleep, or by an external stimulation when someone else awakens him from sleep, similarly one gets awakened from the Big Sleep either by external stimulation or it happens on its own when the sleep is saturated.

In the case of an awakening by external stimulation, he would either be awakened with all freshness, or he would still keep drifting back to sleep or wanting to sleep more. This again depends on how well he has slept. The saturation of sleep is evidently a crucial factor even in cases of awakening by external stimulation. I wonder if anyone would dare to go off to sleep, the very sleep that is most dear to all, if he felt any uncertainty about his awaking after a short rest.

When you resonate with the same frequency as Brahman, or you exist as Brahman, or when Brahman alone is in reality, you are as a still lake and everything else is the waves caused in its stillness. When a granule of sand is dropped on it, ripples originate and dissolve into it. Or maybe you are like the ocean in reality where the waves originate and dissolve into it. Similarly, in the state of Brahman you alone exist without any second. Everything originates in you and everything dissolves in you.

The Gayatri Mantra

Om Bhur Bhuva Svaha
Tat Savitur Varenium
Bhargo Devasya Dheemahi
Dhiyo Yo Nah Prachodayat

Translation:

When consciousness in stillness expands into the infinity of the universe
That is the one which is adorable and illumines all
By meditating upon that effulgence
Be that effulgence by Divine Grace
It is then that the intellect is enlightened

Some of the various meanings of each word of this mantra are:

OM → Brahman, from where the first vibration originates, Vibration of manifestation, First sound at the time of creation

Bhur → Earth, Body, Tamas, Morning, Gross etc.

Bhuva → Atmosphere, Mental sheath, Rajas, Noon, Subtle etc.

Svaha → Beyond atmosphere, Spiritual sheath, Sattva, Evening, Causal.

Tat → That is the one which

Savitur → Illumines all, Brightens up, Illuminates

Varenium → Is adorable, Is respectable, Is the one to be bowed down to

Bhargo → *Illumination, Effulgence, Lustre, Destroyer of sins*
Devasya → *Divine Grace, Divinity, Supreme Lord*
Dheemahi → *Meditate on, Contemplate upon*
Dhiyo → *Intellect, Bhudhi, Understanding*
Yo → *Who, Which, May this light*
Nah → *Our*
Prachodayat → *Enlightens, Inspires, Requesting, Praying*

Elaboration:

The Gayatri Mantra describes that state of man when he is one with Brahman. However hard you try, the limitations of communication through words and language do not describe the experience. Now, in these experiences there are no two i.e. there is no experiencer and the experience existing separately! Even saying 'attaining that state' is actually wrong as 'who' attains 'what', as there are no two. There is only one! All we can say is that when the veil of the non-existing 'ego self' or ignorance present in the mind is lifted or removed, that is the realization of illusory existence of the ego self, and the mind reveals the already ever-existing state. One abides as Brahman itself and is spread out to the expanse of the universe into infinity.

Here, the Atma tattva is in full expanse extending from inside of man into the expanse of the whole of earth, the whole atmosphere, and then beyond the atmosphere into infinity. It is this Atma tattva called Brahman that is the potential power of all manifestation. It is Brahman that illumines even the all-illuminating sun. It is Brahman that illumines even the eyes that see the illumination of the sun. It is the illumination, lustre or effulgence that is behind the working of everything you see. It is in this conscious state of existence that man finds himself to be the embodiment of all knowledge, with the intellect having been illumined. The intellect of man in this state is illumined by Divine Grace, Guru tattva or Brahman. This is the state in which man finds himself to be the knower of all true knowledge. To put it more accurately, man finds himself to be the knowledge itself. In this state he has no doubts regarding anything, anymore. He has a crystal-clear vision of everything. By chanting this mantra, the one who contemplates and meditates on this state would create a transformation within him to this state; rather the state of existence.

What is the best way to contemplate or meditate on this state? Firstly, by using your mind to think or imagine this state. The state of man described in the Gayatri Mantra is a natural state of existence, not a state of meditation or contemplation. You exist in that state. Even the statement that 'you exist in that state' is wrong, as there is no separate 'you' and 'the state'. You are that state!

The natural state is one that happens. The state arrived at through effort is when you imagine it. Even to imagine this state without the imagination going haywire is very difficult. This would require a high level of purity. Only someone who is pure can have a pure mind, and only a pure mind would be a stable one that could imagine that state.

First of all, practice and attain a pure state of mind.

Secondly, contemplate and meditate upon the fact that you are the soul.

Thirdly, when you are stabilised in this state, meditate on yourself as the soul in full expanse as Paramatman or Brahman.

Fourthly, it is in this stable state that Divine Grace showers upon you to illumine the intellect fully and lead to the state of enlightenment.

Anything that we strongly imagine can turn into reality provided it is done selflessly with a pure heart and a pure mind. Such practice over a period of time may result in its happening. Even if the happening of this particular state does not occur, there would be a definite improvement in the intellect due to the vibrations created by the mantra when it is chanted in the prescribed manner.

Commentary On Isavasya Upanishad

I am elaborating on the few lines of Isavasya Upanishad as has been requested.

Om isavasyamidam sarvam yatkiñca jagatyam jagat
tena tyaktena bhuñjitha ma grdhah kasyasvid dhanam.

isavasyam – He resides, the Ultimate Truth resides. For easier communication one can say 'Brahman/Almighty'; so Brahman resides.

idam sarvam – in all this

yatkiñca – in all that you can perceive, as well as in all that's beyond your perception

jagatyam jagat – both; the one from which the jagat (universe) has originated, as well as the jagat (universe) itself

Tena – by Him the Almighty

Tyaktena – whatever wealth is given to you

Bhuñjitha – you may enjoy

ma grdhah – do not crave for

kasyasvid – anyone else's

dhanam – wealth

Isavasyamidam sarvam yatkiñca jagatyam jagat – Meaning:

He (The Almighty) resides in all that you can perceive as well as in all that's beyond your perception i.e. in both: the one from which the jagat (universe) has originated, as well the jagat itself. This means there is nothing and nowhere where he is not! Ponder awhile on this: jagat – all that you can perceive. Where is this jagat? When you are in deep sleep, this world including your body is not there for you, is it? When you are awake the world including your body is back.

Did not the world including your body subside into the stillness of consciousness? And did not the world including the body arise from and with the movement or vibrations in the consciousness?

Or if you like it stated more simply: What was not there when you were in deep sleep, and what is back when you are awake? Is it not your consciousness or the *bodham* that went away and came back? The world is in your consciousness and if the whole world is in your consciousness, then what is the expanse of your consciousness? Is it not all-pervading?

It is in the purest state of consciousness, in that stillness with awareness, that you know Him, the so-called Ultimate, or whatever name you like to call Him. The usage of the words 'that you know Him' is strictly speaking incorrect due to limitations of the language. Actually there are no two, there is only One. You and Him do not exist separately.

tena tyaktena bhuñjitha ma grdhah kasyasvid dhanam –
Meaning:

By Him (The Almighty), whatever wealth is given to you, you may enjoy. Do not crave for anyone else's wealth.

This means whatever is given to you, He is in all that and you are to enjoy seeing Him in all that is given to you without any discrimination. If this be the state, why would you crave for what others have?

Let us understand this further.

Dhana is all that is given to you for your experience, or for you to enjoy. What is dhana? All that you earn by doing good karma is dhana. By doing good karma you earn punya (reward), and by doing bad karma you earn the *paap*. All the happiness you get in your life is the result of punya earned by you, and all the sorrow and pain is the result of paap (bad karma) earned by you.

Now how to enjoy this dhana – both good and bad results of one's karma? It would be more appropriate to use the word 'experience' instead of 'enjoy', and also more appropriate to use 'all that comes into your life' instead of 'dhana'. This experiencing of all that happens in your life is to be felt without any attachment.

Enjoyment or rather experiencing of whatever comes as your share of dhana, all have to be enjoyed and experienced only with renunciation or non-attachment, as unrenunciated enjoyment or experiencing leads to creating strong impressions that lead to furtherance of the soul into future births.

You have to let go of all that is your share without attaching yourself mentally to any of it. Enjoying all that is given to you without any mental attachment is renunciated enjoyment. An apt example is that of King Janaka who outwardly enjoyed all the privileges and luxuries, while also performing karma as part of his kingly duties. However, internally, he always remained attached to the Ultimate.

This is also in conformity with what the Bhagavad Gita says on not desiring the fruits. You have control over your actions but you have no control over the fruits, whatsoever. You are bound to accept whatever you get. You have to undergo, experience, enjoy whatever comes to you seeing 'Him' in everything. Dealing with happiness is not a problem for anyone. Dealing with sorrow or pain is what one has to be careful about. If one starts thinking why this tragedy is seen only in my life... why my brother, neighbour, or friend, who is so much like me in every aspect, is not facing as many problems as I am, or if one holds a grudge against someone who has been instrumental in causing trouble in his life ... such a person accumulates a lot of mental pain nursing such thoughts. This creates strong impressions in the mental sheath, which later on become the reason for continuously being trapped in the cycle of birth and death. Thus, one realizes that whatever comes as one's share in life is the best thing that can ever happen as your accounts get cleared only by that alone and not by what others get in their life.

So what is the point in craving for or desiring what others are seen to be getting? This is the reason why the

Upanishad states that you enjoy what is given by Him to you without attaching yourself mentally to anything. You are to undergo both pain and pleasure without getting mentally attached to either, and thus not creating any impressions in your mind.

Explanation for Stanzas 9, 10, 11, 12, 13 14, of Isavasya Upanishad (not in that particular order)

9. All who worship what is *avidya* (ignorance) enter into blind darkness: those who delight in *vidya* enter, as it were, into greater darkness.

12. All who worship what is not the true cause (manifested) enter into blind darkness: those who delight in the true cause (unmanifested) enter, as it were, into greater darkness.

The Ultimate Truth is as described in Stanzas 4, 5, 6, 7, 8. Everything else amounts to ignorance. Everything else is the knowledge of the manifested, the law of nature, how it functions, the law of causation and its effects and so on. Those who know all about everything at the level of ignorance are no doubt in the darkness or ignorance. And those who know all about the Ultimate Truth, the knowledge of the True, what do you think they are in? Are they not in even more darkness? What is the point in knowing unless you are 'That'? If you are in ignorance, you might stumble upon the Truth someday yourself, and you might be chosen to receive Divine Grace and be in that state. The very knowledge of all truth at the intellectual level is the biggest stumbling block in being 'That', the

Ultimate, as by knowing about this you would always have the desire somewhere deep inside you, and this desire itself becomes the biggest hurdle.

Unless everything inside you is not flushed out, unless you are totally hollow and empty, unless you are totally desireless, unless you as ego disappear totally, this Ultimate cannot happen. This information of the Absolute, this very knowledge of the Ultimate state will always leave a subtle desire in you, a subtle hope, that someday this state might happen to you. This hope, this desire will never let you ever reach that state of total blankness, emptiness or hollowness when Divine Grace showers on you. It is on the showering of Divine Grace that the darkness or ignorance is removed.

This is the reason why the Isavasya Upanishad declares that the one who knows all at the level of ignorance is in darkness, and the one who knows all about the Ultimate is in still greater darkness!

10. One thing, they say, is obtained from vidya; another, they say, from what is avidya. Thus we have heard from the wise who have taught us this.

13. One thing, they say, is obtained from knowledge of the cause; another, they say, from knowledge of what is not the cause. Thus we have heard from the wise who have taught us this.

Avidya helps in purification. Knowing all about the manifested, its laws of causation and effect, and practicing them in your life lead to the purification and further, depending on how strongly you hold onto them and practice them, under testing times you attain maturity.

It is on such a mature soul that the Grace of God dawns leading to the effulgence of the true vidya. It is from this vidya, which dawns upon you by the Grace of the Divine, that immortality happens.

11. He who knows, at the same time, both knowledge and no-knowledge overcomes death through no-knowledge, and obtains immortality through knowledge.

14. He who knows, at the same time, both the cause and the destruction of the perishable body overcomes death by destruction of the perishable body, and obtains immortality through knowledge of the true cause.

The knowing of avidya, all that pertains to the level of ignorance i.e. all about how nature functions, the laws followed by nature, the laws governing all causation and effect thereof and so forth; he by practicing all in accordance with the laws of nature reaches a state where he finds himself in utter darkness when he realizes whatever he has known, learnt, practiced, attained, are all of no use to him; have no ability to save him.

This is the point when everything is flushed out of his system leaving absolutely nothing. His ego-death occurs at this point when this total surrendering to the Divine takes place. The surrendering leaves no trace of himself, and the Divine takes over completely. This is how he overcomes death and goes beyond death. It is then that the truth shines upon him and there is only knowledge (vidya) without the knower. It is this knowledge that reveals the immortality of the Self.

To summarise the six stanzas, the Isavasya Upanishad is explaining the holistic process of Self-Realization.

Firstly, one should have the discrimination between righteous and non-righteous. This knowledge of the righteous and the non-righteous comes under avidya, which is all knowledge that is not of the Ultimate, the Eternal, the non-changing Brahman. Anything that is not Brahman is at the ignorance level, pertaining to that of the manifested. All that is manifested is *maya* (illusion) and therefore non-existent.

All knowledge pertaining to it is at the level of ignorance. It is on the basis of knowledge of the laws of manifestation that one does all his good karma or Dharma, which includes all thoughts, words, and deeds. Even if one is doing his Dharma perfectly, is he not in darkness? By darkness I am referring to all that ignorance until one is realized as the Almighty Brahman. So long as one has not realized the knowing that Brahman alone is and nothing else is, one is in darkness. Only when Brahman remains as the only one without a second, then alone is the darkness removed. Now, if one knows all that is knowable of Brahman without realization, imagine what would be his state. He would no longer have the inclination to do his karma.

Since he knows all about Brahman, he will foolishly manipulate his karma to his whim and fancy. He will take refuge in the qualities of Brahman that there is nothing that is righteous or non-righteous as per the standpoint of Brahman. This is just one example. He is likely to pay no heed to avidya once he intellectually knows the superiority of vidya to avidya. If one who is not realized foolishly leaves all that is of avidya, where would he be?

The fact is if he is not in constant proximity to a Sadguru, he is likely to be greatly confused. And even if by the Grace of the Guru all confusion is removed it is very likely that he will develop a huge ego, which would be very difficult to overcome. Here again, he will need a Sadguru who would keep a constant watch on the ego of his disciple and, whenever the need arises, he on his own instinct would keep shattering the rising ego of his disciple. At this point, the disciple may leave the Guru and free himself into the world doing more harm to society than himself.

This is the reason why Guru bhakti is of utmost importance. This is why the Guru would make sure that his disciple, in truth, has the required faith rather than blind faith in him. Only after doubly ensuring this will the Guru ever shower his grace on the disciple. This is the reason why the disciple has to keep serving the Guru until the Guru is pleased, and it is not easy to please a Guru. The Guru by testing his disciple is actually ensuring the safety of society and the upliftment of the disciple. All this takes him through a tremendous purification process and finally raises the soul to maturity when it is ready to receive Divine Grace.

Sometimes in the process things turn out to be such that all that he learnt, all that he practiced, all that he attained, everything and anything is just not capable of helping him anymore. He is shattered to absolute nothingness. This is when his death happens – a total death when he knows not whether he is alive or dead. This is when he goes beyond death. Death cannot touch him anymore and at this juncture total surrendering happens and the Divine takes over fully. This is the point when the vidya, true knowledge of the Ultimate, dawns upon him. This is when he realizes himself to be immortal.

Explanation for Stanzas 15, 16, 17, 18

15. The door of Truth is covered by a golden disk. Open it, O Nourisher! Remove it so that I who have been worshipping the Truth may behold It.

16. O Nourisher, lone Traveller of the sky. Controller. O Sun, offspring of Prajapati. Gather Your rays; withdraw Your light. I would see, through Your Grace, that form of Yours which is the fairest. I am indeed He, that Purusha, who dwells there.

17. Now may my breath return to the all-pervading, immortal *Prana*. May this body be burnt to ashes. Om... O mind, remember, remember all that I have done.

18. O Fire, lead us by the good path for the enjoyment of the fruit of our actions. You know, O God, all our deeds. Destroy our sin of deceit. We offer by words, our salutations to you.

Verses 15 and 16 are very clear. Still here are a few explanations. The golden disc is the region at the middle of the chest, slightly on the right and on the lower side, being the spot where you concentrate and where the formless and timeless reality reveals itself.

The region at the middle of the chest. slightly on the right lower side, is the spot which is being addressed by different names – the Atma tattva, the Guru tattva, the Witness, the powerful Effulgent One, the Knower.

The power of this tattva is so brilliant, so overpowering that this over-flowing brightness (this power is the mind) itself becomes the shield in not enabling the realization of this Truth. This realization is essential as only this will reveal to you that this unmanifested life is the one which animates not just this physical form, but all physical forms and separation. Only this realization can take you beyond the veil of ignorance, beyond the veil of form and separation into the Oneness.

Verses 17 and 18 speak of that situation when your prayers for the realization of Truth are not fulfilled in this physical form in which you desired. Then the best possibility is stated therein. When the real death or the ego-death happens and the body still lives, we call it as Truth Realization. When the death of the body happens without realizing the Truth, then the best thing one can do is stated in Stanza 18. When the death of the body happens, the mind remembers all that one has done in his life. Here we are talking of someone who could neither realize the Truth in his lifetime, nor at the time of his death. Of such a person, it is expected that the acts he has performed in his lifetime are righteous.

Now, the prayer is to the mind to remember all the deeds that one has done in his life. It needs no reiteration that the deeds that have been undertaken ought to be righteous. The mind by remembering all its deeds would accordingly choose its place of birth where conditions are congenial for its furtherance of 'rest of the spiritual journey', so as to complete its journey of reaching the realization of Truth.

'The sin of deceit' is specifically stated to be the 'Non-Realization of Truth' i.e. that of ignorance of the veil of form and separation. It is advised to pray to the unmanifested life in you to destroy the sin of the veil of form and separation, the cause of manifested life. Only on the removal or destruction of this veil of form and separation would the realization of Oneness happen. Therefore, this is the right prayer at the time of leaving the body, as such a prayer will help in the fulfillment of the desire to realize the Truth at least in the next birth. Because whatever is the last thought at the time of death will bear fruit, or will be the prominent thought embedded in the consciousness in the next birth.

Arunachala Padikam – Verse 6

Q: *I have not yet understood the significance of this verse by Sri Bhagwan Ramana Maharshi: Verse 6 from Arunachala Padikam.*

"Lord of my life! I have always been at Thy Feet like a frog (which clings) to the stem of the lotus; make me instead a honey bee which (from the blossom of the Heart) sucks sweet honey of Pure Consciousness; then shall I have deliverance. If I lose my life while clinging to Thy Lotus Feet it will be for Thee a standing column of ignominy."

What is the significance of the honey bee and the frog here?

Rajini: *Lord of my life!* – is the external Guru Arunachala which is Lord Shiva Himself, and is also the internal Guru which is the Self itself!

I have always been at Thy Feet – Sri Bhagwan Ramana Maharshi is at the feet of Lord Arunachala who is Shiva Himself.

Like a frog (which clings) to the stem of the lotus – Sri Bhagwan Ramana Maharshi compares himself to a frog and compares Lord Shiva or Arunachala to the lotus.

Make me instead a honey bee which (from the blossom of the Heart) sucks sweet honey of Pure Consciousness – Sri Bhagwan Ramana Maharshi pleads to Lord Shiva as Arunachala to make him a honey bee instead of a frog, as a frog can only cling to the stem of the lotus, whereas the honey bee can suck the sweet honey. Here, Sri Bhagwan Ramana Maharshi compares the sweet honey to the Pure Consciousness.

Then shall I have deliverance – Sri Bhagwan Ramana Maharshi says that only by sucking the nectar, which is Pure Consciousness, from the lotus which is Shiva Himself, as the magnificent Arunachala, shall he have deliverance.

If I lose my life while clinging to Thy Lotus Feet it will be for Thee a standing column of ignominy – Sri Bhagwan Ramana Maharshi lovingly tells Lord Shiva or Arunachala that if he loses his life while still clinging to the Lord's feet, it would bring personal dishonour to Lord Shiva and in order to avoid that the Lord should raise him to the level similar to that of a honey bee, so that he is able to suck the sweet honey which is Pure Consciousness.

CHAPTER 11

Process Of Self-enquiry

Self-enquiry or Atmavichara

Q: Sri Bhagawan Ramana Maharshi frequently told questioners: "Look who is asking the question". Does this mean looking inside from the standpoint of the I, or trying to look at the I from inside? Please clarify.

Rajini: When you have a problem, ask yourself 'who' is having the problem. Your mind immediately starts seeking the answer but it invariably gets stuck, unable to pinpoint it. Can you feel that 'stuck mind' unable to move, not knowing 'who' is having the problem when the question is stressing upon 'Who'? This 'stuck mind' is what you have to catch hold of. That is the glimpse you get of the 'no-mind' state. The mind is unable to move, stagnant and stuck. Feel this answerless, stuck or still mind, as the question is thrown at you either by somebody or yourself. That is what you have to capture.

Maybe you will get just a glimpse of the blankness for a second or so, but that's the instant you are not to miss. The more you do this, the more glimpses you will get. But if a mature soul does it, the happening that many crave for will usually happen instantly and effortlessly.

For the mind to be still and unwavering for even a second, one needs a pure mind. To be established in that blankness, it needs to be very, very pure. The purer the thoughts, the thinner the mind, and the easier for it to enter the 'no-mind' state. To give an analogy, this is just like a speeding vehicle that cannot be halted by braking suddenly, as this would cause it to overturn. So, before applying the brake one has to slow it down.

Satsangathwe Nisangathwam

Q: 'Satsanghathwe Nisangathwam,
Nisangathwe Nirmohathwam,
Nirmohathwe Nishchala thathwam,
Nishchala thathwe Jeevanmukthi.'

These are four lines from Jagathguru Sri Sankaracharya's 'Bhaja Govindam'. What could be implied by these lines?

Rajini: If one is constantly attentive to one's inner core (satsangh – in the company of the truth within you), you lose attachment to everything else (*nisangathwam*) – a natural result of being in satsangh.

If one is so disconnected with everything else, he becomes desireless *(nirmohathwam),* which is a natural outcome of nissangathwam.

If one is in a constant state of *nirmohatwam,* the mind, in every minute of life, is found in its state of *nishchalatatwam* i.e. stillness. This is a natural state of effortless Samadhi. And in this state of natural Samadhi, when one is seen to be like a normal person involved in the mundane activities of life, but internally in stillness for every second of it in an absolutely effortless manner, that is the state of *jeevanmukthi* (liberation, salvation).

What exactly am I?

Am I the feelings, or the one who feels? I am not the one who feels, but the one who witnesses both the feelings and the feeler. I am not the one who sees, but the one who witnesses both the seer and the seen. I am not the one who hears, but the one who witnesses both the listener and what is heard. I am not the one who analyses, but the one who witnesses the analyser, the analysed, and the analysis. I am that power that witnesses the power with which everything works. I am that still, potential power which is powerless and witnesses the sprouting of the power with which I am rendered powerful!

Am I this body?

No, I am not. I am the potential power witnessing the sprouting of power creating everything around, including my body. Am I limited in this body? No, I am not.

Am I the mind?

No, I am not. I am the one who witnesses both the coming of the mind and the stillness of the mind. I am the witness of its creation, as well as its dissolution. Everything originates from me, and everything dissolves into me. Everything that originates from me is all me, and all that dissolves into me is all me. All are waves originating from me and vanishing into me. I am the witness.

There is only me and nothing else. I am all and all is me. I witness the creation of ripples in me and the dissolution of them in me. The ripples take a course before they dissolve; the waves take a course before their dissolution. Each ripple or wave is different, though each originates from me. Each has a course different from the other. Whatever be the course, there is an inevitable dissolution into me for another one to form. The course of the next one is formed by the course of the previous one. The strength and direction of the previous spot in the course of a wave, decides the strength and direction of the next spot in the course of the wave.

This is a play that goes on forever and some part of me is unaffected in the depth of the ocean called 'me'. Some are superficially formed waves, some are big and some are small, some are powerful and some are playful, some are useful and some destructive. All are just words. It's all 'me' with no dualities in it.

Now, think of the state when each ripple or wave starts thinking of itself as a separate entity. Is that not ignorance? What is bringing about this ignorance?

Again, it is my own waveform called the mind. The mind-wave, the moment it originates from me, brings in ignorance. The mind is a powerful tool as it is only the mind which has the capability to render itself into its own powerful form. The mind's potential form is its own form in full expanse, into infinity. This happens when the mind is still. Using the mind narrows me down. The more I see myself being used by it, I witness that I am being narrowed down to nothing; a mortal being.

Am I not eternal and am I not all? Am I not untouched by anything and everything? What can touch me at all is only 'me'. I am in all and all is in me. Isn't that true? Am I subject to birth and death? No, I am not. I am the one who watches all beings created from me, and being dissolved into me. I am just 'am', that's all and nothing else. No adjectives, no verbs, no conjunctions, no prepositions, no exclamations; rule out sentences altogether. Only 'Me'!

The wave, what one calls as 'me', in the ignorance caused by the mind (again a wave of 'me'), exists in the ignorance of being separate as an individual and decides its course. In the process, it defines and creates its destiny. Depending upon the course it decides for itself, it reaps what it sows. The sowing could be in a spot of the wave, and the reaping could be at any spot after that, in that wave. That is to say, the sowing could be at a time in one birth, and the reaping could be at any moment after that. It could be in the very next moment, or it could be in the next birth, or at a later time. The wave, believing itself to have a separate identity, chooses the course of 'i' using the mind.

The mind being the cause of all ignorance sees everything in duality and starts choosing. Depending on the choice it makes, it reaps, which again is perceived by the very mind that chooses and finds what it reaps to be of the same quality as the duality that it chose at the time of sowing. That is, whatever was the choice this 'i' made for itself receives the harvest in the very quality of the duality that it chose at the time of sowing. This 'i', in the trap of the mind, is continuously in the cycle of cause and effect. The 'i' chooses and reaps and, at the time of reaping again, it further sows and reaps. This on-going process continues forever and the 'i', unable to escape from its own trap, suffocates.

This 'i' can only escape from the vicious cycle in which it is trapped, the vicious cycle of birth and death, life after life, if it realizes the cause of it being in the trap of its own mind. It is only by using this mind that it can ever realize this truth.

It is only by using this all-powerful mind that this small, powerless 'i' can realize its own all-powerful majestic form of 'I'. The realization that the Truth lies beyond the mind and not within the mind, makes the 'i' wonder how to go beyond the mind. The ways are many but the best way is to plunge deep down to where there is no turmoil and current, deep down where you do not feel the waves, where there is only peace, tremendous peace. Swim when you wish to the depth, or to the surface, realizing that all is you. Understand that these truths will remain within your mind. To experience it all, simply close your mind. The moment all thoughts vanish, you will experience the expanse, the bliss, the eternal peace; you will experience who and what you truly are. You will experience that you and I are one.

Have you tried to experience how you feel with no thoughts churning in your mind? Just try it. See for yourself, feel the stillness! Feel it! When you feel from the centre of 'i' (ego) you feel pleasures and pain, heat and cold, love and hate, being big and being small; in short, everything you feel is in duality. When we exist as the 'I', the real 'me', and feel from there, no dualities are there, only peace, blissful peace is there.

This is a matter to be truly felt. A state of ego-lessness! For the real 'I', there is nothing to do, it is always free and liberated.

What we think, say, and do are the actions of this small 'i' and the reaping of it is automatic. That is what people call fate. By understanding the laws of nature, the 'i' can mould the course of its fate or destiny. This guidance, to be always righteous in our actions, leads us on our journey from the 'i' to the real 'I'. This is a slow method, whereas diving deep into the ocean is the fast method that is meant only for the strong-hearted and those who have tremendous amount of courage.

Let me now address an important aspect of life and how the world refuses to see the Truth. We are seeing ourselves in bondage because of our mind. We do not remember our past-life relationships for the reason that we do not find ourselves bonded with them. The disappearance of memories erases all bindings with so-called 'our own people' even in the same birth.

The entanglements are to be opened and set right, and then this right understanding starts working wonders. We had discussed 'who I am' and 'why I am here' and what caused my appearance here. In the process of understanding this, you also understood the existence of the small 'i' due to the ignorance caused by the mind. You also realized the need of undertaking the journey from the small 'i' into the real 'I' using the mind, to go beyond the mind, towards realization of the real 'I'.

The World is a Projection of the Mind

Q: Unlike the dream analogy, how come all minds see a seemingly consistent world? The hypothesis that 'World is Mind's Projection' is often made in most literature related to the process of Self-enquiry. On analysing, it appears that it is not the mind but the Self that projects the world. Could a clarification be given on this?

Rajini: Your doubts have raised two questions. The first one is: If the world is the projection of our mind, how come all our minds are projecting a seemingly consistent world?

Your second question is: On analysing it appears that it is not the mind but the Self that projects the world.

As to your first question, is not the 'dream state' too offering a seemingly consistent world as in the 'waking state'? Let's take an example: If you and your friend are taking a stroll in a beautiful garden in the 'waking state', I agree that both of you will experience a seemingly consistent world. If in your 'dreaming state', you and your friend are taking a stroll in a beautiful garden, are not both of you in the dream, as in the waking state, experiencing the same seemingly consistent world?

When you consider the example of the 'dream state', be fully there! At the time of dreaming you are not aware of your 'waking state' or the so-called reality. You have to analyse the situation being in the 'dream state' alone, while considering the example of the 'dream state'. Only when you wake up can you say that the dream was inconsistent.

So the 'dream state' too is offering a seemingly consistent world as is the 'waking state'. Then you should not have any difficulty in accepting the example of the 'waking state' as much as you are able to understand the example of the 'dream state'.

Now regarding your second question: On analysing, you conclude that it is not the mind but the Self that projects the world. You are right, but your belief that this derivation is against your understanding that the world is the mind's projection, is to be corrected by right understanding.

Here, understand that the mind is like a mirror that reflects the Self, and the reflected world is seen by you. When the mirror-mind is removed, nothing is reflected and you cannot see the world. So, understand the crucial position of the mind when the absence of it leads to the absence of the world. And under these circumstances, it will not be inappropriate to say that the world is the mind's projection.

Always bear in mind that these are examples given by those who have experienced this, and are only put forth out of sheer compassion for those who want to sincerely know what they have experienced. Such examples are only pointers towards those experiences and are not the experiences themselves.

Absorption of the Mind into the Source

Q: *Although I am aware of the Self-enquiry process and its working, I still have a lingering question in my mind. Most times I feel that I am in a Manolaya rather than in any better state described in the books. At first I was searching for something with my mind and very soon I came out of that bias. Now although I am not 'searching', I am attempting to become aware of 'Who is looking? Who is hearing? Who is thinking?' which arrests my mind to some extent. Is this what needs to be done?*

Rajini: Yes, This is exactly what needs to be done. The claim here is that when such a mind is kept in observation, in short time gaps and then for longer time durations, under continued, sustained observation, it gradually 'dies'. Then this implies that the Source is ultimately exposed. That is perfect.

Q: *Now, for the second part of my question. Is there a 'willingness' factor of the Self or God that comes into play. If so, what is the effect of any effort by an individual? One can spend an entire lifetime on simply observing one's mind while 'willingness' may not be 'showered' even in the next few births. Does spiritual knowledge get carried across several births?*

Rajini: Perhaps I can clear your doubt through an example: Imagine you are at a small roadside teashop. You are having tea there and you notice fresh *bondas* kept there. You feel like having a bonda and you extend your hand to take one. It is then that you realize that there is a transparent, clean glass case which you did not see. Your hand hits the glass and not the bonda. Now, for you to get the bonda the glass cover has to be lifted. When the glass cover is lifted, you can pick up the bonda.

Now, there is another man who passes by the teashop. Would he get the bonda when the glass cover was lifted? No, because he was not there when the glass cover was lifted.

In this example, you may substitute the bonda with *Sat*. You having gone to the teashop and extending your hand towards the bonda is like the effort you put in towards the realizing of Sat, and the lifting up of the cover of the glass case was the Grace of the Divine or the Guru, the 'willingness' of Self as you put it.

On the other hand, the man who went past the teashop did not get the bonda/Sat when Divine Grace happened, as the lifting of the glass cover happened when he was not there on the spot. The effort that would have made him present there at that time was missing in his case.

Now, I hope you understand the role of 'Grace' and 'effort' and that both are equally important. Whatever effort you put in is never wasted. All the efforts that you put in definitely get carried across to the next birth and further too.

CHAPTER 12

Some Hidden Aspects Of Life

'Push' – a Tale of Faith under Pressure

One night a man was sleeping in his cabin when suddenly it was filled with light and God appeared to him. God told the man that He had some work for him to do. He showed the man a large rock that stood in front of his cabin. God said that He wanted the man to 'push' against the rock with all his might every day. So the man obediently started doing this, day after day. For many years, toiling from dawn to dusk, shoulders set squarely against the cold, massive surface of the unmoving rock, the man kept pushing at it with all his might.

Every night the man returned sore and worn out to his cabin feeling that the entire day had been spent in vain. Since the man was frustrated and becoming discouraged, Satan decided to enter the picture and started placing doubts about God's command and other negative thoughts into the man's weary mind: 'You have been pushing against that rock for a long time and it hasn't moved. What have you accomplished?' Thus, he kept insinuating to the man that the task was impossible and that he was failing at it. He then also told him, 'Why kill yourself over this? Just do as you've been told but put in just the minimum effort; that will be good enough.' So that is what the weary man planned to do, but before doing it he decided to put his troubled thoughts to the Lord in the form of a prayer.

'Lord,' he said, 'I have laboured long and hard in Your service, putting all my strength to do that which You had asked. Yet, after all this time, I have not been able to budge that rock by even half-a-millimetre. What is wrong? Why am I failing?'

The Lord, roused to compassion at the man's distress, answered kindly: 'My friend, when I asked you to serve Me and you accepted, I told you that your task was to push against the rock with all of your strength, which you have done. Never once did I say that I expected you to move it. Your task was just to push and keep pushing. Now you come to Me with your strength spent, thinking that you have failed. But is that really so? Look at yourself! Your arms are muscled and your back is strong and brown; your hands are callused from constant pressure, your legs have become hard and massive. Through opposition you have grown, and your abilities now surpass those that you used to have. True, you haven't moved the rock. But your calling was to be obedient and to push; to exercise your faith and trust in My wisdom. That you have done. Now I, My friend, will move the rock.'

Commentary:

At times, when we hear a word from God, we tend to use our own intellect to decipher what He wants, when actually what God wants is just simple obedience and faith in Him.

This man believed that by his efforts he would be able to move the rock and kept pushing with all his might. As time went by, a moment came when he realized that no matter what amount of effort he put in, he would never be able to move the rock. He could not see what else he was unknowingly achieving through his efforts. So, discouraged, he went to God. This going back to God after realising the futility of all his efforts was the real surrender. This is the 'surrendering' that leads to the showering of God's Grace.

The moment you realize you are powerless, the surrendering happens; the 'you' completely disappears. It is then that He takes over. This is how you realize your true 'Self'!

A Poem of Henry Wadsworth Longfellow
with Commentary

A Psalm of Life

Tell me not, in mournful numbers,
Life is but an empty dream!
For the soul is dead that slumbers,
And things are not what they seem.

Life is real! Life is earnest!
And the grave is not its goal;
Dust thou art, to dust returnest,
Was not spoken of the soul.

The poet tells us not to tell him in sad words that
life is illusory, a dream only, that there is nothing called
soul and all that exists is this body and its plight. Though
this is what appears to be the reality, it is something else.
He then tells us that life is in fact real and earnest, not a
dream or slumber. By saying so he stresses on the existence
of the soul very affirmatively, for soul alone is real. He
also says death is not the purpose of life and it is only the
body, which came from dust or matter, that goes back to
it; not the soul.

Not enjoyment, and not sorrow,
Is our destined end or way;
But to act, that each to-morrow
Find us farther than to-day.

110

Art is long, and Time is fleeting,
And our hearts, though stout and brave,
Still, like muffled drums, are beating
Funeral marches to the grave.

Life is neither about enjoyment nor about sorrow. Enjoyment and sorrow have actually nothing to do with life as they are only the results of our own actions in the past. All that's in your hands is how you act now. He further says the acts should be such that they take you further ahead. Whatever be the level at which your soul is now, your acts should be such that they take it to a higher level.

He further says that time keeps moving and although our spirit maybe willing, the body is weak, it is slowing down, and we are just passing through life towards death.

In the world's broad field of battle,
In the bivouac of Life,
Be not like dumb, driven cattle!
Be a hero in the strife!

Trust no Future, howe'er pleasant!
Let the dead Past bury its dead!
Act,—act in the living Present!
Heart within, and God o'erhead!

Here, the poet speaks of life as a battlefield and asks us not to be like cattle just moving about among the herd.

We should not be mindless followers; we should be leaders. When comparing life to a battlefield, he is pointing towards the continuous inner conflicts man goes through. When he asks us to be a hero, he wants us to win the battle.

Further in the next four lines, he gives guidelines to help us win the battle. He says 'trust no future'. These are significant words and their deeper meaning is never to take your decisions looking at the results you wish to get. And when he says, 'act living in the present, heart within and God overhead,' he means one should do what is righteous at the moment according to your inner voice or your conscience.

> Lives of great men all remind us
> We can make our lives sublime,
> And, departing, leave behind us
> Footprints on the sands of time;
>
> Footprints, that perhaps another,
> Sailing o'er life's solemn main,
> A forlorn and shipwrecked brother,
> Seeing, shall take heart again.

He goes a step further to show us that looking into the lives of great people would make things even easier for us. We could move towards leading a righteous life as that would give us the strength and courage, and more so an assurance of accessing a life that's sublime at the deeper levels. This would automatically give guidance and courage to others who are losing heart because they are entangled in the complexities of life.

> Let us, then, be up and doing,
> With a heart for any fate;
> Still achieving, still pursuing,
> Learn to labor and to wait.

He finally concludes that all one needs to do are righteous deeds without looking at the results of one's good actions.

Does not this small poem say everything about life in a few simple words? These are words from deep within the poet's core.

The Four Varnas or Castes

One who is aware of only his physical body exists completely in body consciousness. This level of existence maybe referred to as the primitive stage of man. For such a person, life is meant only to fulfil bodily needs. The word for this level is *shudra*. Such a person's soul evolves to the next level when nature bestows on him those circumstances in which he is forced to see beyond the physical body. He understands right and wrong when he is engulfed by painful emotions and realizes that the cause of this pain is his own wrong actions.

This realization brings him to that threshold where he goes a little beyond his bodily needs and starts doing some good karma. But he restricts the good karmas only to such times when he sees that he will derive a direct benefit from doing them. Such an attitude is very business-minded and the term coined for such *jivas* is *vaishya*.

The next level of evolvement is that of a *kshatriya*. At this level, the person receives Divine Grace to the extent that he realizes that doing good must not be just for satisfying personal needs. It has to go beyond to doing good at all times to benefit a larger number of people. Such a person is seen to exhibit the strength and courage to be on the side of righteousness at all times. He fights with his inner bad thoughts all the time and sees to it that he only has right thoughts and performs right actions. Such a person is a fighter and he wins every time. It is this inner fight that gives rise to the *Brahmin* in him.

This is Self-Realization and he is, therefore, the right person to communicate with the Almighty on behalf of other fellow beings as he is closer to God. Society has misunderstood and misapplied this division of man into castes depending on their birth. The circumstance of one's birth does not mean the family into which one is born, but it is the level or stage the jiva is in at the time of his birth. That a Brahmin would be born in a Brahmin family essentially means that he would be born into a family where other such jivas, who are also at that level, would be around to nurture and guide him.

On Children

Children. What are they? Are they our children? No, they are not! They only come through us, but they are neither ours nor do they belong to us. Their physical bodies are in our hands till they are able to look after themselves.

They have their own destinies and are responsible for it because they too, like us, are in the flow of nature. They have taken birth after having chosen their required situations and circumstances for the fulfillment of their souls' wishes.

You are there to do your duty according to what your conscience dictates and to guide them with all the goodness of your heart, but don't expect the results to be according to your wishes. Expectations lead to problems. Guiding your children with good intentions is all that is required. Thereafter, the results should be accepted without putting any blame or making them feel ashamed of their behaviour or actions. If you were in their position, you could be carrying the very instincts and feelings they now have as children. You would then understand how difficult it is to obey one's parents and follow their instructions at times. We as parents must accept them as they are; patiently and lovingly guiding them on the right path. Anything done, which outwardly appears negative like scolding or punishing, maybe considered to set them on the right path. Never give the impression you are rejecting them or discarding them. Acceptance is very powerful. Nothing is more positive than acceptance!

Some points to keep in mind:

1. Full acceptance of everyone – as they are.

2. Create good feelings within you towards everyone at all times.

3. If you receive any kind of negativity, accept that fully realizing that it is not them but their instincts that are acting up.

4. If one is not able to accept people completely as they are, one is virtually closing all doors to any positive change that might come in them through you.

5. Acceptance leads to positivity, if not today then definitely tomorrow, which is inclusive of the period one refers to as next birth.

Transformation

Q: A spiritual teacher tells us: 'Say to yourself that there is nothing wrong within. There is no change, there is no transformation, and there is no improvement that you want within you.' Is this transformation? Does this mean righteous living can be ignored?

Rajini: It must be understood that these words are delivered to those who are spontaneously living a pure and righteous life, as if it were a flow of nature. Whichever level one is at, righteous living should never be ignored by wrongly interpreting the words.

Here, the words point to a strong, one-pointed desire of getting enlightened. It is this desire or longing that has to be dropped. But for this desire, where everything else is perfect, it is then that one misses what is already there. While reading these words one should not interpret or conclude that righteous living can be ignored. Righteous living is life itself. Here, righteous living is taken for granted when the teacher elaborates on the desire for enlightenment, and on the drawbacks of such a desire. It is for a person who is in the state where righteous living is happening in spontaneity that he says there is nothing wrong within. For such a person no change is required, there is no transformation required, and there is no improvement that he may want within him. And 'that' is the transformation.

CHAPTER 13

True Face Of God

Truth

Q: Is it God's purpose to prove to mortals that He is all-powerful and human efforts cannot come anywhere close to Divine powers and invincibility? If that is so, would it be wrong to conclude that God makes ordinary mortals powerless in order to make them run to Him for help and, in the process, maintain His omnipotence and indispensability? Are we to infer that such a God is selfish and His concern is just for Himself and not for his devotees?

Rajini: God is the Truth and this Truth is a timeless, spaceless, causeless, purposeless stillness or the presence. Truth cannot be spoken about, it can only be realized. He is the Ultimate Reality, the Supreme Consciousness, and He is the subject, not the object. You yourself are ultimately God. One should have a clear intelligence to experience this. For those who are unable to understand this formless, timeless aspect of God, our saints and sages have created the objective God with omniscience, omnipotence and omnipresence. All these qualities have only positive connotations. This *sankalpa* of God is created only to uplift His devotees.

For experiencing this one needs to make sincere, dedicated efforts on one's part and also be bestowed with Grace of the Divine. So long as you do not put in such efforts, you will always feel that maybe there was something more that you could have done, and not having done it has led to your failure. Thus, the first thing for Divine Grace to be showered on you is that you should be fully convinced that you have not left any stone unturned in your efforts.

It is not easy to understand the Truth; the only way is by means of one's own realization. As mentioned earlier, it requires clarity of mind at a certain level to even accept such facts when told about them by sages who have already realized the Truth. This clarity of mind can be achieved by doing spiritual practices such as *seva*, japas, pujas, pranayama or meditation. A person who is not willing to do even a simple sadhana or practice will learn about it the hard way by undergoing hardships and facing adverse circumstances in life. It is then that he will, in desperation, run everywhere and do anything, even any foolish thing, told by anyone to him.

You talk about 'God maintaining His indispensability'. This is akin to the sweet notes that arise from the guitar strings questioning the role of the guitar strings! How valid or relevant is the question of the notes, which are vibrations of the guitar strings, to the guitar strings on their indispensability when the existence of the musical notes itself is due to those very strings? Think about it.

Divine Love

Q: I have heard that love is the easiest way towards realizing oneself. What is this love and how can I live my life according to it?

Rajini: Today, when people talk of love or the way each one of us understands love, is that truly love? We are willing to love others, whoever they maybe, only if they cater to our needs. Whatever be the relationship, are we all not doing just that?

People love their spouse, children, and even parents, only if they satisfy or cater to their needs. How can you ever call that as love? Is it not a business – a give and take business? When I say 'I love so-and-so' it means I should be ready to love that person under all circumstances irrespective of anything. This means I should love unconditionally. If you truly love someone, why bother about what the other does or does not do for you?

In truth, most of us only love ourselves. It is our need and its fulfillment that we love. True love is unconditional. You can see glimpses of unconditional love in the innocent love of a child. Even after the child has been scolded or beaten by a parent, after a few moments the child in all its innocence comes and hugs with the very same love that it has always had for its mum and dad. Have you ever noticed the love of a mother for her baby? Does she not happily take every discomfort or trouble to bring up her baby without ever complaining? When love flows unconditionally, only then it can be called true love.

Find out if you can love at least one person unconditionally. Once you succeed in one case, then you can further extend it to two, three and so on until you find you can love everyone unconditionally! That is Divine Love, the only kind of love. Unconditional love leads to purity of heart. Whatever others think, say or do for you, good or bad, you should have good thoughts constantly in your heart towards all. This way you will attain purity of heart and the egoic self will also gradually diminish and vanish, and you will attain the state of selflessness. This will lead to a state of desirelessness, which in turn will lead to a state of unconditional love.

How to Think about and Meditate on a Formless God

Q: I know that the formless God exists. When one thinks of the formless God, how can one be aware of that which has no form?

Rajini: Before I answer your question, let us discuss the various ways by which one understands God in the evolutionary path of man's journey towards Oneness.

1. At first there is no God and only 'I am'. This 'I am' is the illusory 'i' and is comprised of thoughts, whatever they maybe, according to one's whims and fancies. A gradual shift comes when such a one has to undergo painful situations in life. At that time one takes solace in God.

2. One who takes solace in God starts getting the feel of God, and sees Him in the form that is most attractive to his mind. On developing the virtues that are associated with the deity he worships, the mind becomes purer and starts understanding that the various forms of God are all the same. What matters are the virtues these instil in us.

3. This one God is felt to be residing in the heart so one strives to think, speak and do only what is right to keep the abode of God pure. The person feels that this is the highest offering he can make to God. A stage comes when he no longer has to strive hard to keep himself clean and pure, as by now it has become natural for him to think, speak and do good without any struggle.

4. It is at this point, when the abode of God in his heart is always kept pure that the need for a form loses its charm and he feels that God is his own heart. The formlessness of God happens so naturally when the concentration shifts to your heart, which is where you now feel God. Then the testing times come when the person literally has to struggle to hold on to the heart and his voice, the Divine inner voice, otherwise he would find that life seems to be pulling him away from the Divine in his heart. It is here that you walk on the razor's edge and if you succeed in holding onto the Divine in your Self, you attain the state of maturity.

It is at this state that you are ready to receive the Grace of the Divine and reach Oneness.

5. This Oneness is God Itself and nothing else remains. This cannot be understood by the intellect, but when it happens then there is the experience alone without the experiencer.

6. The ultimate realization is that 'There is no God and only 'I', the real 'I', the core, or that both are the same 'I Am'.' The irony is that it appears to be the same stage from which we started from but, in essence, there is no comparison between the two states.

Spirituality

Q: Is there a tool or medium to experience spirituality, if spirituality is beyond mind and intellect to experience 'That'? Without mind and intellect, you tend to become an inert body akin to a machine that responds only automatically.

Rajini: Forget about a tool. There is only the experiencing; neither the experiencer nor the experience exists separately. In olden days, children were taught to count using stones. Stones are not numbers and neither are they essential for learning numbers.

When you transcend the mind and intellect, you are in that Supreme Consciousness and not as an inert body. The power and the awareness are so high that your so-called tools are nowhere near this state.

Silence is the gateway between spirituality and materialism and one has to experience silence, the emptiness, the void, the stillness, to know and understand what is spirituality.

Q: Silence, hollowness, stillness... are these attributes conditioning our mind in pursuit of the ultimate goal? Does 'nadhopasana' take you to the same goal? Are they the same?

Rajini: *Nadhopasana* (*Nadh* – music, *Upasana* – practice with devotion) will help you develop great concentration. Nadhopasana is not the same as silence. Silence is the 'no-mind' state and not a conditioning of the mind. Here the mind does not exist, neither is there a pursuit or any goal. There is only awareness and knowledge, and this is what you can call Brahman. The Bible says, 'Be still and know that I am God.'

Q: But did He stop saying, 'I Am Only That'?

Rajini: In stillness, there is no speaking; only knowing is there. What I understand from your questions is that you are still at the peripheral level of spirituality.

Q: I am still wandering around in the dark in search of the light, or the sound, or any other trigger. That is why all these questions arise in my mind. Karmam, bhakti and jnanam are three distinct ways to reach Him. I am an ordinary man genuinely in quest of an answer to the question 'Who am I?'

Rajini: Stop the searching. Just be aware of the point from where the search begins. Bookish knowledge or that derived from spiritual discourses does serve a purpose, but experience is entirely of a different dimension.

At this juncture, I wish to share a famous Tamil quote: *"Etthi etthi parkkuvorkku etthathirikkum idam".* (Source: *Tamil Siddhar Padalukal*)

This means: "It is that place where the one who seeks out in search would never reach as the very seeking out in search itself moves him away from what he is seeking for."

To explain further: The very point from which one starts the seeking is itself what one is seeking. And seeking out in search would only take one away from that point. Thus, stopping the search alone is the solution for being at the point which one is searching.

Q: I don't believe blindly whatever I read. To experience that one will have to have a laser sharp mind with one's intellect working overtime. This is difficult for ordinary people who are only human. Perhaps this is where Karma yoga can play a prominent role?

Rajini: Preconceived notions of spirituality from our acharyas and scriptures are the greatest impediment in realizing the Truth. Throw out all the debris as that is the greatest obstacle. Approach the Truth with a mind that's like a clean slate. Whatever knowledge one imbibes from external sources is just debris and everything that's imbibed has to be thrown out before Realization can happen. Then the whole body undergoes a complete transformation.

CHAPTER 14

Newness Is Life's Real Quality

Existence in the Natural State

Q: Eckhart Tolle says: 'To offer no resistance to life is to be in a state of grace, ease and lightness. This state is no longer dependent upon things being in a certain way, good or bad. It seems almost paradoxical, yet when your inner dependency on form is gone, the general conditions of your life tend to improve greatly. Things, people, or conditions that you thought you needed for your happiness now come to you with no struggle or effort on your part, and you are free to enjoy and appreciate them.' What do you say?

Rajini: These are again words of a possibly Realized person from his natural state of existence. There is nothing that a Realized person has to do. He simply exists. There is no doership, so he is not doing anything; things simply flow through him.

The moment one starts speaking, the natural state is disturbed and it moves away from 'what is'. The most effective communication then is only through silence. When we speak of this state, we should bear in mind this limitation. It is only when silence starts communicating that one realizes the inability of language to communicate. No communication is as powerful as silence when it comes to the natural state, because the state itself exists in silence. In silence the I remains in peace doing nothing, whereas the body and mind being part of nature are in their natural flow; an effortless and unresisting flow.

The next line that says that this state is no longer dependent upon things being in a certain way means that this is an unconditional acceptance of what comes, irrespective of whether it is good or bad. When you do not accept unconditionally, whatever is resisted will persist. Therefore when there is complete acceptance without resistance, though it may appear paradoxical, the general conditions of your life tend to improve greatly.

For existing in this state, Divine Grace has to dawn upon you. Even to intellectually understand this state, one needs to be a mature soul. These words on the natural state are not for anyone and everyone. These words usually come spontaneously from a realized soul for a matured soul, depending on the queries that arise from such a soul. For most others, the words arising from someone existing in the natural state simply fall on deaf ears and go unheeded. There is always a shortage of souls capable of receiving what comes out of the existential state of a realized soul. The words that come out from the realized soul could be from the level of existence in the natural state, or they could come from a level lower depending on what is the questioner's level of evolvement. Some realized souls only speak from the level of the natural state, irrespective of the level of the questioner. Whereas some, out of sheer compassion, depending on the level of the seeker, come down to his level, hold his hand and lift him up from that level. If the soul is a truly ripe, mature soul, such words can cause an instantaneous shift into the natural state.

Newness is Life's Real Quality

Q: Quite often I feel bored of life. Why is that so?

Rajini: Everything about life is new and newness is its real quality. Nature takes care of everything. It flows through you. So enjoy seeing it unfold and welcome what all it brings; enjoy seeing how nature handles it through you. That's life! Boredom is a thing of the mind. Get rid of the barrier that hinders the enjoyment. The mind defines and removes the element of enjoyment from most of one's life! Enjoy the company of your own Self, the core of you! It rejuvenates, energises, keeps you filled with contentment, and leaves you blissful. After all, what is there to see, hear, or know outside of you? Nothing at all! Go outwards only to the extent of that what is required for interactive purposes.

Death is the most beautiful happening in life, and when the real death happens you go beyond death, and it is then that you enjoy this uninterrupted free-flowing life. The way an infant sees is truly seeing. We all see with our minds, and it is the mind that creates our world. In fact, we are capable of bypassing sight too in order to see what we have created. The blind too have their own world. Have they ever used their eyes to see? Have not their worlds been created by their minds?

Imagine a lady is waiting at the doctor's for her appointment and four men are sitting in front of her. One is her son, the other her husband, the third is her father, and the fourth is her brother. Now she is one and the same lady, yet all four of them have a different picture of her. For each one of them, she is very different from what she is for the others. Our mind has the ability to create anything and everything, and has the ability to transform everything to anything.

Artificial Life

Q: If life or consciousness can indeed be reproduced from matter, then can consciousness still be considered as the basic building block of everything around us?

Rajini: Consciousness and matter are one and the same. They are simply different vibrations or frequencies of the same 'One'.

A pulsating interchange from the manifested to the unmanifested and vice versa is a constant process in nature. When we call consciousness as the basic building block, it implies that the gross comes from the subtle, but this does not mean the gross does not revert back to the subtle.

After all what is spirituality all about? Is it not reverting back to pure consciousness while still in the gross? It is precisely a transition from the gross to the subtle, subtler and the subtlest, which is the pure consciousness where matter no longer remains and pure consciousness alone is there.

Q: Can you explain, 'Consciousness and matter are one and the same and they are simply different vibrations or frequencies of the same 'One'?'

Rajini: Imagine a still lake. If you drop a grain of sand into it, ripples will be formed. They will appear moving in circles, one by one, ever changing, and they will dissolve or disappear further into the stillness of the lake. Similarly, consciousness manifests itself into the gross, which is ever changing and dissolves or disappears back into consciousness. In the natural state, there is no mind; the experience alone remains.

Q: Does the guitar string change when it produces different notes, or does the water change when different ripples are formed?

Rajini: As long as the essence has been caught hold of, it doesn't matter what words you prefer to use. Even for understanding these matters intellectually one needs to have a clear intellect, otherwise they are not easy to grasp. A clear intellect is obtained by purifying the mind. The purer the mind, clearer the intellect will be.

Purifying the mind is very simple. If one is determined to think good, speak good, and do good, the mind will automatically get purified. To succeed in one's efforts to think good, speak good, and do good is the best that anyone can do. The rest is all a happening of Divine Grace.

Q: If Brahman is one 'without a second' then everything including the vibration or frequency does not exist. Brahman alone exists. What you call as vibration too is Brahman. So don't you think it is more correct to say 'Everything is Brahman' rather than 'Everything is a vibration of Brahman'?

Rajini: You are correct and in reality the difference which you feel is not there in essence, but only in the way one looks at it.

It is one's choice to look at the ripples as water and deny the ripples as if, in effect, they are not there for the very reason that you cannot catch hold of them. You cannot catch hold of them due to the fact that they are ever changing. On the other hand, if you wish to see it all as vibrations of the water, then also you are right.

A particular statement is made for a particular mind at a particular level, and another mind at a totally different level catches it. That statement was made for the initial questioner and it did open up the knot in him. For another person it could be irrelevant and the fact is that for any argument there is always a counter argument, unless you are in the silence, absolute silence, which is a 'no-mind' state.

The 'Now'

Q: What is the 'Now'? I find 'Now' is the 'in-thing' in spirituality whereas it is not found in any of our scriptures.

Rajini: 'Now' is nothing but Brahman! You can discover it for yourself by simply pondering over it. There has never been a time when there was not the Now, nor will there ever be a time when there is not the Now. So then, is not Now eternal? And what is eternal is nothing but Brahman.

The only moment available is Now and there is nothing else.

In other words, Now is:

1. Going beyond time, because in the Now there is no past and future.

2. Going beyond the mind, as the mind dwells only in the past and the future.

3. Existing in the soul consciousness, as when you go beyond time there is no mind and body.

4. It is eternity, as the Now has been there at all times and will be forever.

5. It is the deathless state, as eternity is deathless.

6. Last but not least it is the fearless state, as in pure soul consciousness there is no ego and without ego what is there to fear?

After knowing this, don't you think that there is no scripture or shastra that has not spoken of Now? Because Now is nothing but Brahman.

Q: We can't point out Brahman as a particular entity. Whatever we imagine about Brahman is not Brahman, because it is the witness to our imagination and to our definition. Isn't that so?

Rajini: You are right in what you say but if you understand the essence of that communication, such arguments would not confuse you.

Any words spoken on 'beyond the mind' state can be argued upon endlessly. Therefore silence is the only perfect language at that point. The role of words comes in only when then there is genuine doubt or a knot in the seeker's mind. The words flow out and the effect of those words is the removal of those doubts or knots – or the silencing of those vibrations in that particular mind.

Q: 'Vibrations' and 'Silence' are factors relating to the personal and universal mind. Once your mind gets dissolved in Brahman, that's it. That is 'avaakmaanasa gocharam', which means it cannot be understood by the mind or by any other thing. Am I right?

Rajini: You are absolutely right.

Q: The essence of 'Now' brings peace and happiness. I have many a time witnessed this. But after a few moments, feelings of joy and sadness enter sometimes. Knowing that one is in the present moment, is there a need to disassociate with such feelings?

Rajini: It is evident that the state witnessed by you is not a one hundred percent thoughtless state. Had it been so, the answers to the query would have been different.

So, the next best state for you is to just be in the present moment. This implies not letting your mind drift into the past or the future, but to remain grounded in the present. In this state one doesn't get affected either by the experience of joy or pleasure, or sorrow and pain. One always remains poised, undisturbed, sensible, alert, irrespective of the circumstances one is placed in. One always remains calm, at peace.

The experience of joy and pleasure, sorrow and pain happens when the mind drifts into the past and future and away from the present moment, or what is called the Now. To give an example, just think of a situation where a mother sees that her child has met with an accident. She immediately takes him to the hospital, giving the child courage, strength and loving care along the way. She doesn't even for a second think what would happen if, God forbid, her child would be lost to her forever. She is not crying, panicked, or gripped by anxiety. This is all because she is focused only in the Now – the present moment. If her mind had drifted into the past or even the future, all negative thoughts and emotions would have engulfed her.

The crux of the matter is moving away from the present moment into either the past by thinking about how it happened, why it happened, who caused the accident and so on. Or, projecting the mind into the future and thinking what would happen now, will my child survive or not, and even if the child survives what permanent damage would be caused and how she would manage to cope with such a situation.

One should be alert and not let the mind drift away from the present moment. Let every moment play itself out and be there fully. A deep level of peace will then descend upon you. The present is all there is.

Q: When people are quite well settled... I guess financially secure... they also realize that there is no time, so they need to live in the NOW and all that... But what about the person who has no food to eat, what about the person who is worried about passing 10th standard, getting a rank in competitive exams, getting a good job with a good salary etc.? I am here referring to the general public.

Rajini: Being well settled has nothing to do with knowing oneself. The kind of knowing that you feel comes naturally after Self-Realization. This wisdom grows from inside and it doesn't have an outside source. This knowledge comes spontaneously.

Do you think all Realized souls have attained that state after studying and knowing about everything? One need not go and study anything for this. There are two things about Self-Realization. One is that Self-Realization is a happening, and it happens by Divine Grace. Secondly, although it's true that it's a happening, one needs to be mature enough to receive that Grace. So, all one has to do is be ready to receive the Grace when it dawns upon you.

Live a righteous life. Live it according to your inner voice. Whatever sincere effort you make in this direction will not go to waste.

CHAPTER 15

Beyond The Mind State – An Online Conversation

An Online Conversation

Q: Do you agree that the world is all in the imagination or mind, as is said in the scriptures?

Rajini: When the mind subsides, what world can exist?

Q: Then the world is not there for you?

Rajini: Yes and no.

Q: When you have the world, is your mind creating it?

Rajini: Yes. When the mind is closed there is no world. When you use your mind, the world is there and that too is an illusory world where you communicate and interact.

Q: In that case, my mind created you?

Rajini: Yes, your mind created me. You have to know all this not just intellectually but in reality, at the existential level.

Q: When I sleep there is no world for me?

Rajini: That is correct. But what you have to experience is the 'no worldliness' even when you are awake.

Q: So whatever you are saying to me, my mind is telling me in your voice?

Rajini: Not just what you hear or see while we are talking; also your own thoughts, and you as you know yourself today – it is all your creation.

Q: Out of compassion, you as my creation, are now speaking to me?

Rajini: If you want to know about the world, you have to first know your Self. Once that is known, nothing remains and there ends the whole story.

Q: Are you me?

Rajini: Why do you want to know about this state? It is not possible to know about this state unless you experience it, as the tool that you have is only the mind with which you cannot comprehend anything. It's only when you go beyond the mind that you can comprehend about this state.

Q: You are answering my questions. Does that mean you are creating me, or am I creating you? Then we must be one. Still your experience is not mine. Why?

Rajini: These questions are not being answered by me; the answering is only happening. You see me as this body but I am not that. Neither are you that body, and nor is it any different from me. Everything is a flow of energy. Everything flows out of me and since you are only seeing yourself as the smaller self, you don't realize that everything is actually flowing out of you too. You and me are in essence the same. The only thing you have to do is to realize that. It is just as the water of the ocean is not different in the two waves that are created from it.

Q: So we are one in a broader perspective only. Now we are two?

Rajini: As long as you do not realize yourself, who you really are, you will keep on clinging to you and me as two. Once the wave knows that it is of the same water as the ocean, how will it differentiate between the other wave, and that wave itself? So, realizing oneself leads to the realization of the eternal Oneness.

Face To Face With Reality

Q: Then what is the point in saying you have known and I have not?

Rajini: I am not saying that, your questions and doubts are saying so. There is essentially no difference between you, me, a worm, the tip of a blade of grass, or the galaxy! In fact, there is nothing called Realization if you want to hear the truth.

Q: Isn't there an illogical kind of logic here?

Rajini: Yes, you are coming nearer by saying it is illogical logic. When you speak of the truth it evaporates at that very moment, and what can be somewhat closer to it is when you say both the opposites.

Q: By knowing the knower all will be known. Is that true?

Rajini: Yes that's it, and that is all.

Q: This is out of curiosity… do you know me?

Rajini: I need not know you.

Q: But you must! Because you know yourself and all that should be… even I should be known to you. Am I not right?

Rajini: You are known as well as unknown to me, but there is no need to know you.

140

Q: From the known point, can you say what is the colour of my shirt?

Rajini: All that is there is me, and my energies are ever changing and always in flux. Change is the nature of my manifestation, so there is no question of knowing anything that is ever changing. You are trapped in your mind and so are the questions that arise from that state. Colours, as well as all that your sense organs perceive, and all that your mind perceives, are limited. As long as one identifies oneself with limited factors, one is trapped in them and so would be the questions. You are beyond all that and that is what you have to realize. Your curiosity can only lead you outwards. So long as you don't go inwards nothing can be known. How do you know what you see is right and anything I tell you is not? You are capable of perceiving only what your sense organs are limited to see. One may tell you the colour of your shirt is blue and the other may argue it is black, looking right at the shirt.

Q: Please tell the colour a normal man may say... whether it's red, or black, or don't know!

Rajini: You want an answer? It is, 'Don't know!' Do you know there are loud noises all around you? Can you hear them? No you can't, because those are limitations of the sense organs and they have nothing to do with knowing yourself. By knowing yourself, you will realize the irrelevance of your questions.

You are limiting yourself to this body. That is why you have such doubts and ask such questions. The reality is not that. Your body is just like a pebble on the seashore of the real you!

Q: You are the sea, so you must know. Shouldn't you?

Rajini: What do you understand by knowing?

Q: OK. Then can you tell me when I will get Realized from a layman's view of time?

Rajini: You are under the wrong notion that magic has got some role in becoming Realized. I don't do anything, Things just happen. I have nothing to do with any doing although it all originates from me. Why do you want to be Realized? What is wrong with you now?

Q: Nothing...

Rajini: Complete your sentence.

Q: Nothing except physical ailments. But Ramana Maharshi and Ramakrishna Paramahamsa too had painful deaths, so what hope do I have?

Rajini: What do you know of the state that you want to reach, that you long for it so much?

Q: Super human … alpha omega…

Rajini: Your mind created that?

Q: Yes.

Rajini: There is absolutely nothing. When there is no mind, how can there be anything? So all you need now is that you don't suffer from physical and mental pain, isn't it?

Q: Yes.

Rajini: For that, realize what is causing it and remove that.

Q: What is the cause of abdominal discomfort? The mind? So one must end mind when there is pain?

Rajini: All you can do now is to stop thinking. If that's not possible, stop thinking of stomach pain. If that's also not possible, divert your attention. And if that also is not possible, observe the pain without defining it mentally. Try to catch hold of the pain, concentrate all your attention on the exact spot of pain. If even that is not possible, you can tell your mind that your stomach is in perfect condition and that there you are in perfect good health. Positive thinking too is miraculously powerful.

Q: That I tried, but I lacked conviction!

Rajini: What kind of conviction was required?

Q: I was in pain and I was saying I am well, knowing it was a lie!

Rajini: How does it matter as long as the pain is relieved? You wanted the pain to suddenly vanish and if it vanished in this way, how does it matter?

Q: It didn't happen that way. I saw a doctor, took medicine and now I'm slowly getting better.

Rajini: That is alright. You may take medicine or see a doctor.

Q: But I do not want the pain to happen.

Rajini: This wanting, resisting the natural flow, is the cause of all pain. When we start accepting all that happens, there is no pain. When you fall down you resist and break your bones, but when a baby falls there is no resistance and so it seldom gets injured.

Q: Can you touch fire and not get burnt?

Rajini: The essence is not that, it is the pain that you feel; the difference is in that.

Q: Yes, I understand... you are indifferent to your body.

Rajini: As you said earlier, Ramana Maharshi and Ramakrishna had a painful death; according to you that is. But that was not their experience.

Q: Whatever happens, happens... yes ... I too want to reach that state.

Rajini: There is no short-cut method. There is no method for Realization. It is a happening, but the happening cannot happen to anyone who is not ripe enough, and ripeness starts only when one is pure enough. For purification and ripening there are methods and paths, and that process has already been explained to you.

Q: Yes, a pure mind...

Rajini: Yes, and that process need not happen in the same birth.

Q: I have seen one person who is 80 years old; his name is Shivetta. He said he was Realized. If he's really Realized what will he think of me?

Rajini: He will not think of you, and not just you, he won't think about anything.

Q: Ok. So whatever I do will not offend a realized man?

Rajini: Yes, but you will have to be prepared to bear the consequences of your actions at the hands of nature. He will not do anything but nature will take its toll on you.

Q: Do you think everything happens due to God's Will?

Rajini: Yes, but it is not my thinking. It is the truth!

Q: So all that happened to me was of God's Will?

Rajini: That's true, but as long as you are in the shell of your mind it is not so.

Q: You are safe… for any question you have this fantastic answer!

Rajini: You are right, the end of knowledge is Realization. What do you know when your mind is closed?

Q: Nothing, it is true, all are thoughts. I must try to remain thoughtless… since there is the possibility of more explanations, I would like to be satisfied.

Rajini: It first requires a thorough cleaning of your mind as you have accumulated a lot of trash in a haphazard way. All that has to be cleaned. The result of storing all this nonsense has resulted in confusion, and this has led to the closing of all doors and things are bouncing back. Do you want me to do the cleaning of your mind?

Q: I don't know. You are Realized, so you know better.

Rajini: I am not the power that works, though it originates from me. I could have suggested it if you had some openness, but it is up to you.

Q: So you are going to leave me?

Rajini: You have the free will to do as you choose. There's no discrimination here.

Q: I hope you are not disappointed.

Rajini: Nothing elates or disappoints me, for I do nothing. I suggest you don't hear words that are transcendental as they would only confuse you. You have to do lot of sadhana before you are ready to understand these matters.

Q: I still want to meet you.

Rajini: You are not yet ready to see or meet me. I suggest you talk to me more frequently. A time will come when you will want to see me from your heart, unlike with just a desire from your intellect, which you have now.

Q: I will wait. I am you!

Rajini: Those are lame words when they come from you – lame and meaningless. It's just like a parrot speaking. Speak from your level, not from what others say.

Q: Sorry, I was just being playful; that's all.

Rajini: I am not saying all this to make you feel sorry. My words are not directed towards that, they are guidelines for you. Be true to what you are; feel that. Don't go by what others say that a Realized soul can or should do. The reality is that you can't comprehend them or their actions as you have only the mind as your tool, and they are beyond the mind!

Epilogue

Telephonic conversation of Rajini with a Swami on 18th July 2013

R: Swamiji, today is a special day. Can you guess what it is?

S: Is it the day of your *Saakshaatkaar* (Realization)?

R: No.

S: Then what is it?

R: It is the death anniversary of someone who was very dear to me.

S: (*Expressing concern*) Who is that?

R: That is Rajini.

S: Hahaha... then who is sitting there? A ghost?

R: All of you think that what you see is Rajini, but there is no one like that.

S: Then why did you say 'No' when I asked if it was your Saakshaatkaar day?

R: How can I need any Saakshaatkaar! In fact, there is nothing called Saakshaatkaar!

Glossary

Adharmic Unrighteous

Advaita Non-duality

Advaitin An adherent of Advaita philosophy

Aham Ego Sense or 'I AM' sense as per usage

Aham-bhavam Ego sense

Atma Infinite Absolute Reality behind the body and the individualised consciousness

Atma tattva Inner Divine

Avidya Ignorance; knowledge of the manifested

Bhakti Path of devotion to achieve God-realization

Bhashya Commentary on scriptures

Bhavam Attitude

Bonda A south Indian snack

Brahman The Supreme Being, the Primal Source, the single Absolute Being pervading the Universe

Brahmin Superior priestly class

Buddhi Intelligence

Glossary

Dharma A set of rules or guidelines to help you realize your true 'Self'

Dukha Sorrow

Dvaita Duality between the perceived subject and the perceived object

Grantha Religious book; sacred text

Guru Spiritual teacher

Isavasyamidam sarvam God resides in the entire universe/everywhere

Japa Chanting of mantra

Jiva Individual soul

Jnanam To know oneself or realize oneself

Karmam Past action

Kshatriya Warrior

Manasakshi Inner voice

Manolaya Concentration, temporarily arresting the movement of thoughts

Marga Path

Maya Illusion

Mithyatva Illusory

Paap Sin; bane

Paradharma Partaking of the nature of Kshetra in which he resides

Prakruti Nature or manifested

Prana Life force

Pranayama The breath control exercises of yoga to gain mastery over the Prana

Puja Worship of God, usually in the form of an image

Punya Good Deeds; Boon

Purushartha Efforts

Sadhanas Spiritual practice

Sankalpa Conception or idea or notion formed in the heart or mind, solemn vow or determination to perform, desire, definite intention

Sat Truth; Unmanifested

Satsang A sacred gathering; in the company of the truth within you

Seva Service to Guru

Shakti Divine feminine power

Shastra Scriptures

Shishya Disciple

Shiva Truth

Shruti The body of sacred texts comprising the central canon of Hinduism and one of the three main sources of Dharma

Shudra One who is predominantly in body consciousness

Sukha Pleasure

Swadharma My righteous duty

Swaroopa My true self

Tapasya Ascetic discipline

Tattva Principle; Element

Vaishya One who is business-minded

Vasana Instincts/tendencies

Vedanta End of knowledge, when Realization dawns

Vidya Knowledge of the Unmanifested

Yagna Ritual sacrifice usually for specific objective

Readers may contact the author via email:
4trueseekers@gmail.com
to seek guidance on moving smoothly
in their spiritual pursuit.

For further details, contact:
Yogi Impressions Books Pvt. Ltd.
1711, Centre 1, World Trade Centre,
Cuffe Parade, Mumbai 400 005, India.

Fill in the Mailing List form on our website
and receive, via email, information on
books, authors, events and more.
Visit: www.yogiimpressions.com

Telephone: (022) 61541500, 61541541
Fax: (022) 61541542
E-mail: yogi@yogiimpressions.com

 Join us on Facebook:
www.facebook.com/yogiimpressions

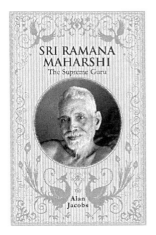

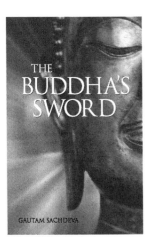

The Sacred India Tarot
Inspired by Indian Mythology and Epics
78 cards + 4 bonus cards + 350 page handbook
The Sacred India Tarot is truly an offering from India to the world. It is the first and only Tarot deck that works solely within the parameters of sacred Indian mythology – almost the world's only living mythology today.

Made in the USA
Middletown, DE
06 October 2020